ABOUT THE AUTHOR

Tendayi Viki is an award-winning author and innovator. He has worked with several large organisations including AkzoNobel, Air France, Lufthansa AirPlus, Pearson, Standard Bank, Salesforce, Unilever, Rabobank and TD Ameritrade.

Tendayi co-designed and helped implement Pearson's Product Lifecycle, which is a lean innovation framework that won Best Innovation Program 2015 at the Corporate Entrepreneur Awards in New York.

Originally from Zimbabwe and now based in London, Tendayi was shortlisted for the Thinkers50 Innovation Award and named on the Thinkers50 2018 Radar List of emerging management thinkers to watch (www.thinkers50.com). He is the author of two other books: *The Corporate Startup* and *The Lean Product Lifecycle*.

ABOUT THE ILLUSTRATOR

Holger Nils Pohl is a visual strategist – his core strength is creating clarity and helping companies design a better future. He has worked with companies such as Zurich Insurance, Roche and IKEA.

Holger helps clients create lasting strategic solutions rather than quick fixes. His clients say that he performs magic with his visual imagination.

He's the founder of the WorkVisual Institute, lecturer at the MHMK Cologne and the UdK Berlin. Holger is a co-creator of the business game Playing Lean and author of *Creating Innovation* and *Biz4Kids*.

> **With special thanks to the Ignite Team
> at De Beers Group**

PIRATES
IN THE NAVY

TENDAYI VIKI
ILLUSTRATED BY HOLGER NILS POHL

First published in 2020

Unbound
6th Floor Mutual House, 70 Conduit Street, London W1S 2GF

www.unbound.com

All rights reserved

Text © Tendayi Viki, 2020
Illustrations © Holger Nils Pohl, 2020

The right of Tendayi Viki to be identified as the author of this work has been asserted in accordance with Section 77 of the Copyright, Designs and Patents Act, 1988. No part of this publication may be copied, reproduced, stored in a retrieval system, or transmitted, in any form or by any means without the prior permission of the publisher, nor be otherwise circulated in any form of binding or cover other than that in which it is published and without a similar condition being imposed on the subsequent purchaser.

Text Design by PDQ Digital Media Solutions Ltd.

A CIP record for this book is available from the British Library

ISBN 978-1-78352-894-3 (paperback)
ISBN 978-1-78352-895-0 (ebook)

Printed and bound in Great Britain by Clays Ltd, Elcograf S.p.A.

With thanks for the support of Unilever Foods & Refreshment

With thanks to the super patrons

Rob Aalders
Sumayah Al-Jasem
Joachim Allerup
Broos Bakens
Hubert Bannel
Carlos Barahona
Ludovic Belz
Abdullah BinSabbar
Stefan Blaser
Celia Bohle
Jean-Marie Buchilly
Thomas Buesch
Henrik Byremo
José Calado
Ana Patricia Carvalho
Pavel Chunyayev
Justin Coetsee
Alfredo Colombano
Sam Conniff
John Crawford
Timothy Daniel
Amelie De Spot
Franck Debane
Clément Demaurex
Jesse Desjardins
Michele Di Marino
Richard Ebner
Kristian Elmefall
Frederic Etiemble
Viktoria Fagerfjäll
Matt Fante
Otto Freijser
Maciej Gawlik
GED Testing Service
Christiane Gerigk
Hardy Gieldanowski
Ilya Gogin

Sarandos Gouvelis
Ben Hafele
Chris Henderson
Carol Hill
Maartje Jung
Adam Kaye
Maj-Britt Kjær Sørensen
Joost Korver
Maarten Korz
Ronald Kriedel
Jonas Kristjansen
Sebastian Krumhausen
Arve Kvalsvik
Ove Kvalsvik
Alain Lafourcade
Alan Langman
Andrew Le Roux
Marcus Liehr
Christophe Lutz
Kristian Thorsted Madsen
Ole Madsen
Farai Madzima
Paulo Malta
Terence Mauri
Mathieu Menet
Anna Mezyk
Pascal A. Miserez
Laurens Molegraaf
Per Christian Møller
Lauris Muzikants
Carlo Navato
Darlene Newman
Kenny Nguyen
David Nosibor
Peter O'Shaughnessy
Jesper Oelert-Pedersen
Zoltán Paksy

Peter Pascale
Giorgio Pauletto
Guillermo Lorbada Rodríguez
Matthieu Salles
Jan Schmiedgen (co:dify Group)
Bianca Schmitz
Dan Sears
Jeroen Smith
Yves Stalgies
Henry Stewart
Craig Strong
Jen Sutherland
Mihai Svasta
Andy Thomas
Paris Thomas
Dan Toma
Ilya Tulvio
James Twigger
Pascal van de Poll
Ferry van Halem
Guy Van Wijmeersch
Michela Ventin
Camillo Weinz
Frank Wubbolts
Nick Young
Betsy Ziegler

Contents

INTRODUCTION: More Fun to Be a Pirate   1
CHAPTER 1: Be the Change   5
CHAPTER 2: The Innovator's Choice   27
CHAPTER 3: A Little Humility   55
CHAPTER 4: Start with Discovery   67
CHAPTER 5: Start Small   83
CHAPTER 6: Repeatable Process   107
CHAPTER 7: The Catalysts   135
CHAPTER 8: Scale the Movement   153
CONCLUSION: Not All Pirates Are the Same   167
EPILOGUE: An Underground Movement   171

Introduction
MORE FUN TO BE A PIRATE

When Steve Jobs said that it was 'more fun to be a pirate than to join the navy', he was highlighting the fact that large companies are much slower to respond to change than startups. This is the speedboat versus oil tanker conundrum. The bureaucracy that runs many established companies is inadvertently designed to create inertia. This is not very helpful in a fast-changing world.

Unlike startups, large companies also have to follow the rules. As Steve Blank notes:[1]

> *Startups can do anything.*
> *Companies can only do what's legal.*

Having no business model and no market reputation to defend makes startups quite dangerous as competitors. If you combine this with the fact that startups are now better funded and their incentives are aligned with their investors' goals, large companies are competing with a formidable foe.

Meanwhile, inside most large companies there are still leaders

---

1 Blank, S. (2017). 'Why you can't just tell a company "be more like a startup"', *Harvard Business Review*: https://hbr.org/2017/06/why-you-cant-just-tell-a-company-be-more-like-a-startup

who question the need to innovate. To be fair, there is a discernible shift in leadership attitudes towards innovation taking place in most organisations. However, in some large companies there is still an intractable core of leaders who actively resist innovation projects as a waste of time and resources.

It is a myth that innovation is sexy. In a lot of companies, it is career suicide. So, while startups are focused on resisting enemies and competitors that are outside their company, innovators within large companies have to contend with enemies and competitors inside their own companies as well.

Corporate innovation is a paradox. Intrapreneurs – employees who work on entrepreneurial ideas inside an established company – have to innovate for the future, inside a machine designed to run the current business. It is the management of the current business that tends to get in the way of innovation. The bureaucracy and incentives of the organisation are all geared towards improving and exploiting the currently successful products and business models.

At the same time, these large corporations have entrepreneurial employees who are constantly trying to innovate. As far as I am concerned, these people are crazy. They wake up every morning and go to work to swim against the tide. This is insane! And yet, they exist: passionate employees who are committed to helping their company become more innovative. They can see the future coming and they are committed to ensuring that their company survives in that future.

Only a few leaders are happy with these crazy innovators. The majority of leaders view them as disruptive rebels, aka 'pirates in the navy'. These leaders actively create barriers to block innovation efforts, often driving intrapreneurs to quit their jobs in frustration. When innovation does succeed inside a large company, it is often in the form of one-off projects that have had to be guided through the landmines of corporate politics. This can be demoralising.

Most intrapreneurs recognise that they cannot keep doing innovation as a series of ad hoc projects that have to jump through political hurdles. They realise that there is a need for some changes inside their companies to allow innovation to happen as a repeatable process. But how do they get this done? How do pirates in the navy slowly transform their companies to become more supportive of innovation?

This book is written for passionate innovators who are working inside companies, especially large ones. If you have ever asked yourself the questions below, this book is for you:

- How do we get our company ready for innovation?
- How do we change the culture within our company?
- How do we start a movement that transforms how innovation is managed?

- How do we influence our leaders to prioritise innovation?
- How do we work with detractors and naysayers?
- How do we collaborate with enablers such as finance, HR, legal and branding?
- How do we bring about lasting change that sticks?
- We get the theory and we get that innovation is important – but how do we actually get it done in our companies?

I am totally convinced that it is possible for innovators to succeed as pirates in the navy. It is just that their piracy has to become a part of the institutional structures and processes inside their company. I will repeat this point several times in the book: *innovation has to become a part of the institutional structures and processes inside large organisations*. This book will provide innovators with some guidance to navigate the choppy waters of corporate politics, while successfully transforming their companies.

Chapter 1
BE THE CHANGE

Innovation myths

The buzz of innovation is everywhere. The jargon, labs, accelerators, startups – it's hard to keep up. And yet, corporate leaders are slowly waking up to the fact that they may have been victims of innovation myth-making. As much as they have been keen to drive innovation, their actions have been counterproductive because they are influenced by myths about how innovation works. These myths are not just minor quirks in leadership, they can result in serious mistakes that lower company returns from innovation.

Below I will present nine examples of such myths and explain why they are wrong:[2]

- *Adopt the lean startup method and you can always pivot your way to success:*[3] Lean startup tools are about testing and finding out quickly which value propositions and business models might work, and which won't. We should then make decisions about which projects to kill and which ones to invest more resources in. The risk is that we will pivot – or make changes to our business idea – into perpetuity.

- *Let a thousand flowers bloom*: This myth is based on the notion that there is no such thing as a bad idea. This is wrong. I believe that teams should be working on ideas that are aligned to their company's strategic goals and innovation guidelines. If innovators work on any random interesting ideas they like, they will find it much more difficult to get support from their company to scale those ideas.

---
[2] Adapted from Viki, T. & Osterwalder, A. (2019). Busting Innovation Myths: Part 1. Strategyzer: www.strategyzer.com/blog/posts/busting-innovation-myths-part-1
[3] This myth is a major pet peeve of my good friend and bestselling author, Alex Osterwalder.

- *Big returns require big bets*: This myth comes from the idea that innovation is all about investing heavily in technology and research and development (R&D). Innovation is only expensive if you use traditional business planning to make investment decisions. Innovation, if done right, is about making many small bets, testing ideas cheaply and quickly to identify the winners in which you then invest more resources.

- *Innovation is sexy*: Actually, innovation is brutally hard work that often leads to failure. The daily grind of innovation and its iterative nature requires people who are not easily discouraged. In most corporations, innovation is *not sexy* at all. It often spells the end of a promising career.

- *Corporate ventures have more resources*: In today's environment, startups are actually much better funded than corporate ventures. Venture capital is awash with resources that they invest in startups, giving them time to search for successful business models. These resources and the patience required are simply not always available in large companies that are mainly focused on managing existing business models.

- *Money doesn't drive innovators*: The myth here is that innovators just need a cool place to work and an amazing mission. While a great working environment and a wonderful mission are important, it is also frustrating for innovators to create new multi-million-dollar growth engines and not get rewarded for that work. Innovators need to be appropriately rewarded for the value they create.

- *It's all about great ideas*: Companies are constantly searching for more ideas using tools like idea jams, collaborative brainstorming and competitions. This is not enough – ideas are a dime a dozen and just a small part of the equation. Successful innovation is about turning great ideas into a business, with a sustainably profitable business model that can create value for customers.

- *Innovation is about technology and R&D*: While exploring new technologies can be exciting, innovation is much broader. It is about creating value for customers with business models that scale. This is why the Nintendo Wii was able to succeed with less powerful hardware technology, but with a great value proposition (i.e. social gaming in your living room) and a business model that appealed to non-traditional gamers. Innovation based on technology and/or R&D is just one part of overall innovation opportunities.

- *You can't learn innovation*: This is a myth propagated by the press who put successful entrepreneurs on the covers of magazines without highlighting their learning journey and the long trail of failures that usually preceded their success. For example, the founders of PayPal started off working on an idea to transfer money using personal digital assistants (PDAs), before they landed on their now successful virtual payments business model. The truth is that entrepreneurial tools, methods and skills can be learned, especially if we are given the chance to gain experience and practice with real innovation projects.

If only these myths did not affect real decision-making, we would be in a good place with innovation in large companies. However, I have seen leaders make actual decisions based on these myths. The result of this is innovation theatre, which does not produce great products or new revenue growth.

Innovation theatre

Innovation myths are counterproductive because they lead to bad decision-making. Most companies have leaders who truly want to support innovation with the right tools and environment. But their belief in innovation myths results in the creation of artificial practices

that only scratch the surface of what real innovation should be. And so, innovation theatre rules the day. This is a major pet peeve of mine. Some popular examples of innovation theatre include:[4]

- Creating open spaces with whiteboards, bean bags and foosball tables.
- Teams that use loads of sticky notes and canvases.
- The adoption of casual dress, such as jeans and T-shirts.
- Innovation leaders with funny titles like 'Ninja' and 'Sherpa'.
- Using innovation jargon like 'pivot', 'minimum viable product', 'iterate', 'experiment' and 'hypothesis'.
- Accelerators, incubators, labs and catalyst funds.
- Oh and of course, the regular pilgrimage to Silicon Valley.
- And a chef, to make free-from burgers for the hipster programmers.

These practices are not necessarily bad in themselves. Indeed, I have used many of them in my own work with companies. When used the right way, some of these practices work. They only become innovation theatre when they are used without a good understanding of the underlying principles that inform their design.

Corporate leaders have been spending money funding innovation theatre. I have been in many corporations that will proudly show off their innovation spaces, but when I ask about returns from innovation, I am quickly told: 'We are still learning.' And when I ask what they have learned … *nada*.

What I have found most surprising, though, is that leaders are driven

---

[4] Adapted from CB Insights Presents: Corporate Innovation Theatre In 8 Acts (2015). CB Insights: www.cbinsights.com/research/corporate-innovation-theatre/

to invest in this innovation theatre by the so-called intrapreneurs inside their organisations. So, what I have learned is that this is not only a leadership problem, as some intrapreneurs also believe in innovation myths and are unwitting fans of innovation theatre. This has shocked and upset me a great deal.

Such an inauthentic approach to innovation never lasts in the long term. In fact, most innovators find themselves fired from the companies they work for within a couple of years. But the damage they do within companies is actually more long-lasting. Inauthentic practitioners make things harder for future innovators. They make leaders who were already sceptical about innovation even more sceptical than they were before.

So, before we start trying to take on the navy, we need to check ourselves. Who are we really? Are we genuinely knowledgeable and committed to drive authentic innovation practices within our organisations? In other words, why does our innovation lab exist?

Why does your innovation lab exist?

Inspired by the other companies who have done the same and fearful of being disrupted by startups, several companies have opened innovation labs and startup accelerators. However, the success of such corporate initiatives has been mixed.

The question I am often asked is: 'What do you think about innovation labs?' This is a hard question to answer in a vacuum. I try to reframe the question as follows: Why was the innovation lab set up in the first place? What problems were you trying to solve?

Surprisingly, very few heads of innovation I have spoken to are able to provide a clear answer to these questions. Even the people running the lab or working in it struggle to provide clear answers. This is a massive problem!

There seems to be a fear of missing out when it comes to innovation labs and corporate accelerators. Other companies are doing it, so leaders feel compelled to be proactive as well. This leads to innovation labs being set up with a mixture of contradictory objectives that make success hard to accomplish and measure.

Before a lab or an accelerator is set up, clear strategic objectives around innovation must be formulated at the company level. This will provide guidance for what the lab is supposed to accomplish. An innovation lab or accelerator should not be set up until these strategic choices have been explicitly clarified.

If you are a pirate in the navy and you become part of an innovation lab that does not have clear strategic objectives, you will regret it later on. Do not be happy that the company has now given you a place to play. This would be a mistake. A big mistake.

Learning Innovation

The goal of innovation is to ultimately impact the bottom line net profits of the company and help sustain it in the long term. There are companies that have created innovation labs as a way to work with startups, in order to learn about new arenas and industries without investing too many resources. Using innovation labs and accelerators as a form of research about certain industries is a great idea, as long as leaders realise that research and innovation are not the same thing.

The real question is, as we work with startups or internal teams to learn about new industries, how are we going to convert those learnings – what we have found out – into long-term revenues for the company? We have to design our labs and accelerators so that they are able to extract insights and create value. Your job as a pirate in the navy is to show your leaders that you are creating value, not just learning.

Culture Change
Some intrapreneurs I have met claim that the goal of their innovation lab is to change their company culture. This goal can be a good one, but success is much harder to come by. The first challenge is that innovation labs are often set up as physically separate institutions from the main organisation. This separation creates a sense of otherness for both the people that work in the labs and the rest of the company. It is hard to change a culture that you are not viewed as being a part of.

You are now a pirate alongside the navy, not a pirate in the navy.

If the strategic goal is culture change, then the people based in the lab will have to work really hard to connect with the rest of the company. They cannot be viewed as a silo where all the 'cool kids' work and hang out. They have to open their doors and initiate meaningful conversations with the main company. Culture change takes patience and persistence – a characteristic many pirates may not have.

It's a Distraction
Making culture change their main goal can distract the innovation lab teams from the real goal of innovation, i.e. creating new business models and revenues for the company. This is not a trivial concern.

I have worked with innovation teams who were mostly focused on hosting events to drive culture change. But after a couple of years, they found themselves in trouble with their leaders, who were now asking for bottom line revenue impact. Culture change alone is not valuable unless it drives growth.

As I will illustrate later, I have found that the easiest way to change a culture is to achieve early successes and share those stories with the rest of the business. The more successes an innovation lab has, the more convincing their story becomes. Leaders will be resistant to lean startup and design thinking if all we have to show them are sticky notes and canvases. Our work as innovators is to create value for the company. If we fail to do that, our labs will eventually be closed, and the leaders will be absolutely right to do that.

Your boss was right to shut down your innovation lab

As much as innovation labs have been popular, there is also another trend that is being seen more and more, and this one with much less media fanfare. Several companies are quietly shutting down their innovation labs. Over the last few years, I have spoken to various innovation managers who were angry that their company had decided to close down the labs they were running. These managers clearly felt that the leadership in their companies comprised MBA types who 'don't get innovation'.

But when I have drilled down into the work that these so-called innovation labs were doing day-to-day, I have often discovered that it was actually the innovation managers that 'don't get innovation'. While they assumed that they were perhaps too pirate for their

companies, they were actually inauthentic practitioners. It turns out their bosses were right to shut down their labs because:

1. *It wasn't really an innovation lab*: Most people working in innovation labs tend to conflate innovation with creativity. Creativity might be an important part of innovation, but 'coming up with cool ideas' is not sufficient for innovation to succeed. As already noted, innovation is the combination of creative ideas with sustainably profitable business models. If you have one part and not the other, you don't have innovation. A lot of innovation labs are well designed to spark the creative juices of the people who work there with appealing working spaces and idea jams. However, very few labs are designed to search and find profitable business models for the ideas being generated. Creativity labs they may be. R&D labs they may be. Innovation labs … not really!

2. *Lack of strategic alignment:* A lot of innovation labs work on projects that are not aligned to the parent company's strategic goals. The labs are often set up without a clear remit and over the years they shift from project to project without ever really figuring out how they are meant to make a contribution to the

company. This lack of strategic alignment also creates orphans: great new products with a good business model that wither on the vine because there are no managers in the company who are willing to take the product to scale. As pirates, we have to make explicit agreements with leaders about how the company will scale successful ideas from the lab.

3. *Lack of focus*: Without strategic alignment, you get a lack of focus. Letting a thousand flowers bloom is not good for your garden and it's definitely not good for an innovation lab. As already noted, there is a myth within innovation lab circles that 'there is no such thing as a bad idea'. Yes, there is. Bad ideas are those that don't help companies achieve their strategic goals. It may not be a bad idea overall, but it is a bad idea for *your* company. Remember the goal is not just to be a pirate, but to be a pirate in the navy. Innovation labs need to have a strategic focus. This helps with developing knowledge and expertise and stops innovators jumping from one unconnected idea to another.

4. *It's mostly innovation theatre*: I cannot repeat this enough. Pool tables, bean bags, pianos, ping-pong tables, Post-it notes, canvases, copies of *The Lean Startup*, walls painted back-to-back with whiteboard IdeaPaint, posters with Steve Jobs quotes. Then there is the jargon: minimum viable products, pivots, experiments, iterations, customer development, design thinking … blah blah blah. Most innovation labs are trying to channel their inner Silicon Valley. It may look like the design and consulting firm IDEO, but it is not IDEO. It is important to realise that there is a reason behind all the visible things we see great

innovators do. The visible things we see are just expressions of innovation principles. Our job is not to imitate the visible but to understand the underlying principles.

5. *Show me the money*: This is the final nail in the coffin for most innovation labs. A lot of them make zero contribution to company revenues within three years of starting. Ask the innovation managers what they have been doing and they will reel off a bunch of activity and vanity metrics: events hosted, press mentions, experiments run, number of customer conversations, number of hackathons and minimum viable products launched. Number of validated business models? Zero. Number of validated business models taken to scale? Zero. At the beginning of the innovation lab, activity metrics are important. But after three to five years, innovation labs have to demonstrate impact. And the key impact metric is revenue from new, profitable business models.

Enough Already

So as much as I love and respect my innovation lab colleagues and some are doing really great work, I think we need to start looking in the mirror a little bit. What is the point of our work, if it's not to innovate? What is it to innovate, if it is not to build great new products or services with profitable business models? If you find yourself fumbling around for an answer to these questions, then your boss was right to shut down your innovation lab.

But wait, I hear you say. We don't need to create growth and new revenue. What about branding and public relations? There is value in branding and PR, right? What about creating an innovation lab for

PR purposes only? Is this not a good idea? As you might expect, my answer to that question is: no.

Creating innovation labs for PR purposes is bad for innovation

There are a few companies that have set up corporate accelerators and innovation labs for networking and PR purposes only. In some circumstances, the budget for the accelerator program actually comes from the marketing department. Which, in my view, is completely bizarre.

An argument made in support of this practice is that an accelerator can raise the public profile of the company as being innovative. This in turn helps the company to recruit better talent. Accelerators also raise the profile of lean startup methods within the company, especially with leadership at the executive level. This awareness and visibility is assumed to help with the future development of an innovation culture within the company.

In practice, such cultural change rarely ever happens. Most labs and accelerators are islands that are set up and managed separately from the main business. The products they create are hardly ever adopted or taken to scale by the main company. In fact, when you dig deeper, you start to realise that setting up innovation labs or accelerators for PR purposes can actually be detrimental to the innovation culture that you are trying to create.

Why Innovate?
At the heart of this discussion is one important question: what is

innovation for? The reason we encourage companies to innovate is because their long-term survival depends on it. This is why they don't just need cool new product ideas; they need those ideas to be commercially viable. So, a great innovation culture is one in which the majority of innovation projects are aimed at finding this commercial viability.

If an accelerator is set up for PR reasons only, these innovation best practices will not emerge. In fact, most of the startups selected for the accelerator will be based on the ability of the company to use them to tell a great story to the media, versus having real commercial potential. The lab itself will be designed to look like a creative startup space with whiteboards and sticky notes.

Such practices send an implicit message to employees that innovation is about the artefacts that startups use, not the creation of real value. The everyday grind and hard work of innovation is hidden from them; it all looks like fun and games. So, they learn nothing from the concept of having an innovation space.

But wait, it gets worse. There is often an assumption that startups are great at innovation and using lean startup methods. In my experience, this is a myth. Most startup teams that I have met have no interest in lean methods or running experiments. They just want to build their product. You often have to drag them kicking and screaming out of the building to go and talk to their customers. Startups need coaching and encouragement from authentic practitioners. Such practitioners are non-existent in an innovation lab that is set up for PR purposes only.

Then there are the huge egos that the 'visionary founders' develop after being accepted into the accelerator program. They begin to feel that they are there to save the company from disruption by startups. These attitudes irritate leaders, who are only too happy to see these startups leave when the accelerator program is finished. When this happens, the accelerator will have damaged the development of an innovation culture within the company.

Double-edged Sword

The idea that labs and accelerators create awareness and visibility may be true, but this is a double-edged sword. If your accelerator gains the attention of executives in your company, you may celebrate this as a success at the beginning. However, you are actually in more trouble than you think. While the innovation theatre may get you executive attention, it is only the substance of your work that will allow your lab to survive long term.

In the end, executives always ask the bottom line question: How much are we spending on this accelerator and how much return has it produced? And yes, you can claim you are still learning. But even that has a time limit. Eventually, the question will return: what have you learned and what have you produced for the company using those lessons?

Then there is the talent. It is true that companies viewed as innovative can recruit the best talent. This is also a double-edged sword. Great talent that is drawn by the potential to innovate will want to innovate when they join the company. What they may find instead is a culture that is the exact opposite of what they expected. If they are truly talented, they will not hang around for long. And the word will soon be on the street to stay away from your company.

Keeping It Real

What is most frustrating for me is the damage that this does to corporate innovation. There is quite a lot of innovation fatigue among the executives I have met. They all have stories about the money they have spent on innovation labs that created no real value for the company. The blame is put squarely on lean innovation methods, which are then regarded as inappropriate for large companies. It takes a lot to convince these leaders that there is real substance behind all the theatre they have experienced. This is why we have to be authentic. We have to embody the change that we want to see in the world.

Be the change you want to see in the world

To be authentic innovators, we have to be keenly interested in what works. We can't do innovation just for show. Authenticity requires us to take the time to really understand what we are trying to build as a practice for our company. By getting clarity on what a good innovation process looks like, we will then be able to decide how we can bring this to life within our organisations.

Explore – Exploit
The first thing to highlight is that there is a difference between exploiting current business models and exploring new opportunities. This distinction between executing and searching was first noted by Steve Blank.[5] For intrapreneurs, this distinction matters because it lays bare what their job is. While the main business improves and executes on the currently successful products and business models,

---

5 Blank, S., & Dorf, B. (2012). *The startup owner's manual: The step-by-step guide for building a great company. California: K&S Ranch.*

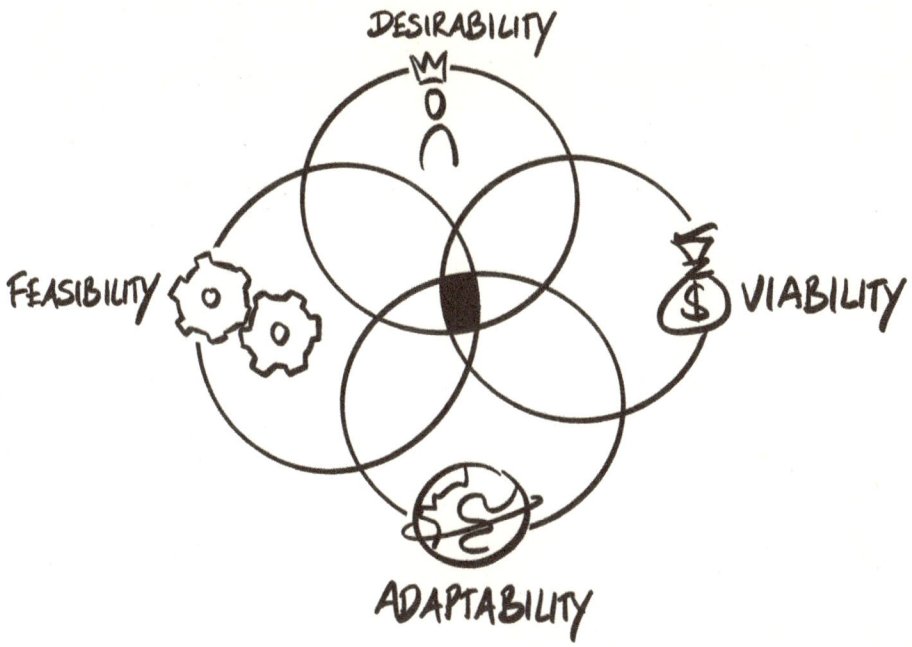

the role of innovators is to explore and search for new, profitable business models.

Please note that I did not say make exciting new products or come up with great new ideas. I did not even mention technology or R&D. While all these things may be an important part of the mix, the goal is to find *profitable* business models. This is what we are searching for as innovators. Which means that our work, tools and methods must be deliberately chosen to support this pursuit.

Searching For Value

As intrapreneurs, we search for value propositions that resonate with customers, and great business models to support the sustainable delivery of this value. Searching is different from executing because it is a nonlinear process. It is two steps forward, one step back and another two steps sideways. It is a lot like solving a puzzle with jumbled-up pieces, and no visual guide to help you.

What we do know from experience is that profitable business models have four key elements or big puzzle pieces that must be solved for:[6]

1. *Desirability:* Making sure that we are making products that customers want and delivering real value.

2. *Feasibility:* Making sure that we have the capabilities in place to create and deliver value to customers.

3. *Viability:* Making sure that the costs of creating and delivering value to customers are less than customers are willing to pay (i.e. profitability).

4. *Adaptability:* Making sure that our business model is adaptive to the business environment and that the timing for launching our product into the market is correct, so we can achieve scale.

These are the major pieces of the puzzle we have to solve in order to find profitable business models. And as you can see, it is not just about ideas, products or technology. Innovation requires that we also pay attention to our value propositions, business models and business environments.

The Right Organisation

The question for pirates in the navy is what sort of organisation do

---

[6] Osterwalder, A. (2017). 'How to systematically reduce the risk and uncertainty of new ideas', Strategyzer: https://blog.strategyzer.com/posts/2017/12/6/how-to-systematically-reduce-the-risk-uncertainty-of-new-ideas

we need to have in place to support innovation? This is a key issue to consider because we want innovation to become a part of the company's structures and processes.

This means that we need to work with leaders to create a clear innovation strategy that defines where to focus. We need to make sure we are aligned with all key functions within the company and be clear on how they can support innovation. We also need to make sure that our leaders are using the right tools to make investment decisions and track the progress of our work. Finally, we need to ensure that our teams are using the right tools and methods for innovation.

As you can see, to be a pirate in the navy means taking the tools of piracy and having them institutionalised as best practice within our companies. Talk about trying to swim upstream! Who would want such a job? But before we get into the details of how this can be done, let us first explore what choices we have to make as innovators.

Chapter 2
THE INNOVATOR'S CHOICE

The myth of the innovation lab

Let's revisit the topic of innovation labs from Chapter 1. I would like to tackle the topic from a different perspective: what actually happens when we are successful as innovators. It is important to recognise that there are authentic innovators out there doing good work. These are hard-working, diligent people who understand how to apply lean startup methods and tools in the right way. They often succeed in creating great products with good business models.

But when they are ready to take their successful products to scale, they face resistance from their company. Wait ... What? Companies resist the chance to make money by launching products with validated business models? Yes, they do. I have seen this with my own eyes.

Innovators are often frustrated by this situation. In fact, it drives them crazy. They have just pulled off the miracle of finding a business model that works, and nobody is thanking them for it. In fact, they are being actively avoided by leaders and moved around the organisation as if they have some communicable disease.

This is puzzling to innovators. Why would corporate leaders fund an innovation lab and then refuse to scale the successful products that are created there? Why waste time and resources in this way?

This is the myth of the innovation lab, the idea that the leaders who funded the lab understand its purpose and support innovation. The innovators working inside the lab assume that their parent company loves them and this lulls them into a false sense of security. What we are learning is that the opening of the innovation lab itself often represents innovation theatre played out at the leadership level within the company.

Being a pirate in the navy means that you must never forget who you are. Don't get comfortable too soon. You are a *pirate* in the *navy*. The navy is still the navy. It is a traditional institution. When the lab was created, the navy was trying to figure out a way to tolerate your pirate behaviours without having to change itself. Until innovation is an institutionalised part of your company, tread lightly and pay close attention to stakeholders – particularly the key players and influencers in the company.

It is very rare that you will find a leadership team that has thought through the implications of opening the lab. The first symptom of this is the lack of a clear innovation strategy. When they set up the innovation lab, they were simply hoping that something that will save the company would emerge from there. But without clear strategic goals, leaders often fail to recognise a good product that may save their company when they see it.

This is made worse if the new products from the lab threaten to cannibalise existing successful core products in the parent company. The instinct to protect those traditional revenues will trump any other decision-making.

A second symptom is the lack of a clear framework for managing innovation. Most companies do not have a method for tracking and measuring innovation success. Furthermore, they do not have a clear framework for taking products from the lab back into the main company or spinning them out into stand-alone divisions. This means that the leadership team are unprepared for managing the challenge of success when it happens. For these leaders, innovation success is actually a problem.

Know Where You Are

What we are learning is that the really smart innovators understand that successful innovation requires them to manage their stakeholders well. The need for mindful stakeholder management is always clear to people who are working on projects within the parent company. In that situation, they know that their project will not succeed without support from key stakeholders.

When the situation changes, and the project is being run in an innovation lab, some intrapreneurs forget the value of stakeholder management. But the most successful innovators know that they still have to manage their relationships with the parent company – even if they are working in a physically separate innovation lab.

The lesson is to not let the creation of the lab lull you into a false sense of security. You are not in a safe space. The navy does not love you as much as you think it does. There is still a lot of work to do to get buy-in, acceptance and support. This is the most difficult aspect of being pirates in the navy. We are dealing with complex organisations. There is always a tension between exploration and exploitation and this creates a paradox that we need to understand in order to make the right choices.

The seven paradoxes of innovation

The first choice you need to make as an intrapreneur is whether you really want to be working inside a company. To help you with this decision, let's quickly dispense with the notion that you can turn a large established company into a startup. A large company is not a startup, nor should it strive to be. This is not the goal of pirates in the navy. If you want to be part of a startup, then you have to go and start or join one.

At the same time, I fully believe that we can help large companies to be just as innovative as startups. But in order to do so, we have to be aware of the paradoxical situation we find ourselves in. This awareness in itself can be powerful and help you to make good choices. Unlike startups, which can focus on the single mission of succeeding with one main idea, large companies have to handle a myriad of competing concerns and paradoxes:

1. *Searching while executing:* It is worth repeating Steve Blank's description of startups as temporary organisations whose goal is to search for profitable business models, as opposed to established companies that mostly *execute* known business models. Blank's distinction is really helpful for startups to understand where they are on their journey. However, the second part of the distinction is only partially helpful to established companies that want to be innovative. For established companies to innovate successfully, they have to figure out a way to be *searching while they are executing*. They have to put the two together somehow. This dilemma lies at the core of all the other innovation paradoxes presented below.

2. *Create new products, manage established products:* Managing established products can be done using traditional accounting methods and metrics such as profits, return on investment (ROI), net present value (NPV) and accounting rate of return (ARR). In contrast, the creation of new products has to be managed using startup methodologies such as experimentation and iteration, and success is measured by how well the innovation team is doing in their search for profitable business models

(i.e. innovation accounting). These two different management practices have to be done simultaneously within the same organisation. This means that our leaders have to know how to run an established company and a startup at the same time. They have to be able to read numbers on a P&L and balance sheet, as well as assess the amount of risk reduction an innovation team has achieved.

3. *Deliberate strategy, emergent strategy:* Established companies have traditionally developed strategy in a top down and deliberate manner. The idea was that the leadership team set the strategy and the employees executed it. In order to innovate successfully, companies have to use a combination of deliberate strategy based on vision and emergent strategy based on knowledge of the market. When teams that are using innovation test their products and business models with customers, the results can help refine their overall strategy. As such, even as leadership sets the course, there should be a willingness to welcome change based on our findings from the market. This is the best way for a company to be adaptive. We need to have strong opinions that are also lightly held.

4. *Decentralised decisions, increased transparency:* The reason why leaders often want to have control is that they may not trust employees to make the right decisions. They may feel they need some control in order to keep employees executing the agreed strategy. But command and control management often stifle innovation, so leaders have to defer some decision-making to innovators. However, as leaders defer decisions to us as

intrapreneurs, we have to create tools that capture the decisions we are making. This means that while our leaders lose control, we provide them with transparency in exchange.

5. *A single company, not a single business model:* In order to innovate, large companies need to stop thinking and acting as if they are single organisations with one business model. Instead, established companies should view themselves as an ecosystem of different products and business models. The complexity of managing several business models at different phases of their lifecycle is now the job of every contemporary leader – and as pirates in the navy, we have to understand this and help make their jobs easier.

6. *Fail fast, make money:* Leadership in established companies is expected to execute well and generate profits for shareholders. And yet to innovate, they also have to willingly embrace failure. Failure comes with costs in financial, physical and human resources. So how can a company fail fast and make money at the same time? The key to managing this paradox is to understand that failing fast is not the ultimate goal. The goal is to use failure to *learn fast*. What we are learning as a company are better ways to make money with better products.

7. *Impatient for profits, patient for growth:* Established companies are often already operating at scale and there is a tendency to want to take new innovative products to scale as soon as possible. This premature scaling is one of the main reasons that innovation fails. Therefore, Harvard scholar Clayton Christensen encourages

leaders to be patient for growth and encourage their teams to pursue profits first.[7]

These are the seven paradoxes of innovation that we need to be aware of as pirates in the navy. We are not in a simple situation where we can just innovate at will. We need to understand that our company is in a bit of a pickle. Our leaders are trying to balance several competing concerns. Running the core business is a valid and important job for leaders to do. Profits from that business are what pays for innovation. This is why our leaders often engage in contradictory behaviours that drive innovators to leave the company.

Ten things companies do that drive their innovators to leave

As much as I have been hard on intrapreneurs and their lack of authenticity, companies also have an innovation leadership deficit. As far as I am concerned, the buck for innovation success ultimately stops at the desk of the CEO and her executive team. It is ultimately their job to create an environment in which innovation can flourish. Our job as pirates is to help them accomplish that.

In order to help our company build a sustainable innovation process, we have to understand what the company is doing to frustrate innovation. This information is useful in helping us to decide what we want to do within the company. Do we really have the

---

[7] Anthony, S.D. (2013). 'The get-big-quick fallacy', Harvard Business Review: https://hbr.org/2013/06/the-get-big-quick-fallacy.

patience, talent and skills to deal with these challenges? Below, I will share ten things I have seen large companies do that may drive you to quit being a pirate in the navy:

1. *Telling innovators to come up with some cool stuff:* This sounds good. Liberating even. But always remember the myth of the innovation lab, especially when leaders don't talk about strategy. What exact kind of cool stuff do leaders think the company needs to meet its strategic goals? Innovators are being set up for failure when leaders say to them: 'Never mind strategy. Just bring me some cutting-edge products and technologies. You are the startup guys!'

2. *The business case:* Innovators can come up with a whole bunch of cool new stuff to work on. But they need a budget. In order to get money, they have to complete a thirty-page business case to justify their proposed project with five-year projections. Business planning does not work for innovation. Five-year revenue projections for new and untested ideas are fiction. Innovators know this, and so does leadership. But it's a ritual we must follow. So if you don't prepare a long business case, no money for you.

3. *Arbitrary decision-making:* Fine. We will prepare the business case. We will also attend the meeting where we pitch our ideas. In those meetings, half the execs will not have read the business case. But these are powerful folks, so they will begin to quiz innovators with random questions. And no … they didn't just ask the innovation manager about strategic alignment. Your colleagues told her last month to ignore strategy and come up

with cool ideas. Executives will fund their pet projects, products they personally like or business ideas that sound convincing. It's hit and miss when you pitch ideas. You have no real clue what idea is going to get money or why.

4. *Sales owns customers – so don't talk to them:* You are one of the lucky few to get money for your project. Now you want to start doing some customer interviews to learn more about customer needs. The sales director is incensed at this idea. Sales owns all customer relationships. Please do not talk to customers without approval from the sales director. But innovation requires that we create customer value, so we can't build our products in a vacuum. Furthermore, waiting to get approval from the sales director slows down the innovation process and limits the number of iterations we can test.

5. *Your minimum viable product will hurt the brand:* Speaking of testing, leadership panics when they see a proposal to launch a minimum viable version of the product to test and learn from customers. The fear is that this will hurt the brand. This is not a ridiculous fear to have, as there are some real risks. However, there are ways to mitigate these risks. Rather than stop experiments altogether, companies can work with innovation managers to set some basic rules as to when and how the company's brand can be used when testing solutions.

6. *Our tech team will only get to that in six months:* No, you can't hire your own developers. Part of the innovation process is building, testing and iterating solutions quickly. In some companies,

software building belongs to the technology department, meaning that all software products must be built or approved by this team. Everybody else must submit their specifications and wait six months while the tech team works through its backlog. This process can be slow-moving and is the antithesis of innovation.

7. *On time, on budget:* If innovators somehow manage to jump through all these hoops, they will then have their quarterly or annual review meeting to talk about progress. If they have new findings that prompted them to change their idea or business model, all hell will break loose. 'Why are you doing that?! It is not what you stated in the plan we approved. All we want to know is, are you on time and on budget? Are you delivering on the plan?' It doesn't matter that the plan had never been proven to work in the market.

8. *Unexpected budget cuts:* The company is not going to meet its projected sales this coming quarter. So to save money, leadership decides to cut the budget on innovation projects. One of the things that makes the startup ecosystem work is that the teams always know how much financial runway they have left. Imagine an investor calling a startup founder to ask for some money back because their fund is not going to meet projections. Ever-changing budgets are not good for innovation.

9. *You failed, you are fired:* Fail fast is a great mantra to speak out loud, but it is much harder in practice. We know that for innovation to flourish, failure must be celebrated within the

company. If innovators see individuals with failed projects losing their jobs, this will create an uninspiring environment. Furthermore, people working on innovation projects will become unwilling to admit failure. This then results in the projects running for longer than they should, which creates unnecessary expense.

10. *Hope you enjoyed the workshop, now get back to work:* To support innovation, a lot of companies are running design thinking or lean innovation workshops. However, even as their employees learn these great skills, the companies are not set up to benefit from them. Most employees find that they cannot apply their newly acquired skills within the company they work for. What is the point of learning about customer development and experimentation, if you are not allowed to talk to customers?

It has become very clear to me that organisational structures and processes have a tendency to overpower human capabilities. Even the most skilled pirates cannot create great new products while doing battle with the navy about innovation processes. In fact, some of these battles can become quite negative and personal, leading good innovators to quit their jobs for greener pastures. This is why our work as pirates in the navy is to help make innovation a legitimate part of the company's structures and processes. But this is really hard work, especially if we have to change the architecture of how our company is run.

Changing the architecture

Xerox invented most of the technologies that we use in personal computing but Xerox is not one of the largest computing companies in the world today. Kodak invented the digital camera and still filed for bankruptcy in 2012. Nokia was one of the pioneers of the smartphone and still lost significant market share to the iPhone.

There is a narrative in the business world that views large companies as likely to get caught out by startups in ways they do not expect. An example of this is the hotel industry getting disrupted by Airbnb. It is indeed true that disruption can come from unexpected angles. However, the companies noted above not only saw the future coming, but some of them invented that future. The question is why did they fail to capitalise on the imaginations of their brilliant teams?

Doing What We Have Always Done
There is something seductive about success. It lures people into doing the same things that made them successful in the past. When a company finds a successful business model, management are given the goal to exploit that advantage to its fullest extent. This means that most companies are structurally organised to exploit their currently successful business model. All the company structures, operations, processes, tools and culture are geared towards doing what they have always done.

This is not necessarily a bad decision. Companies do need to exploit their current advantages. After all, this is where their revenues and profits are coming from. The mistake companies make is in organising themselves to focus exclusively on exploitation. Every business model has a lifecycle. The decline of any business model is inevitable. In fact, business model lifecycles are becoming shorter and shorter.

So if a company is structurally organised around its current business model, this means that the lifecycle of the company is tied up with the lifecycle of its business model. When the business model eventually declines, the company will decline as well. Our job as pirates in the navy is to uncouple the lifecycle of our company from the lifecycle of its business models.

Architectural Innovation

In an article for the *Financial Times*, the Undercover Economist notes that successful companies are more likely to struggle when new innovations require them to change their organisational structures.[8] This inbuilt inertia in organisations was first identified by Harvard professors Rebecca Henderson and Kim Clark, who coined the term 'architectural innovation'.[9]

Henderson and Clark highlighted the fact that what matters is not whether an innovation is breakthrough or incremental. What matters is whether the company's current structures can absorb the innovation and take it to scale. A breakthrough innovation that fits a company's current structures is more likely to succeed. In contrast, an incremental innovation that does not fit into a company's current structures is likely to fail.

The challenge most companies face is that there are very few breakthrough innovations that fit their current structures.

---

8 Undercover Economist (2018). 'Why big companies squander good ideas', Financial Times: www.ft.com/content/3c1ab748-b09b-11e8-8d14-6f049d06439c
9 Henderson, R M. and Clark, K.B. (1990). 'Architectural innovation: the reconfiguration of existing product technologies and the failure of established firms', Administrative Science Quarterly 35, 9–30.

THE INNOVATOR'S CHOICE

Breakthrough innovations often require new and different business models to succeed. This is where misalignment is likely to occur. Since most companies are structurally designed to deliver on their current business model, any innovation that uses a different business model will require some structural changes within the company.

The extent of the required changes and the willingness of the company leadership to drive those changes will ultimately determine the success of innovation. This was the challenge that Xerox and Kodak faced. They had the resources and foresight to develop innovative new technologies. What they seemed unwilling or unable to do was to implement the right business models to take those technologies into the market. This is the challenge we will be facing as pirates in the navy.

Organisational Changes Are Hard

As a practitioner of corporate innovation, I have direct experience of how hard it is to change organisations. Anyone who tells you it is easy has never tried to do it. It is more than just mindsets that need to change. Most leaders and managers now understand the need for innovation. What is difficult is implementing the right structures and processes for innovation to succeed on an ongoing basis. Easier said than done! This is why simply running workshops where we do lean startup training is no longer enough.

Lean startup training is not enough

The Lean Startup began as a grassroots movement within the startup ecosystem. Over the last few years, the movement has developed a powerful toolbox of techniques and methods that help innovators navigate their way towards profitable business models. Noting the success of the movement within startups, leaders in large companies began to take an interest in how they could bring this toolbox into their organisations.

And just like in the beginning, lean startup in large companies often began within the grassroots. Intrapreneurs were interested in getting training on how to use lean startup methods and tools. And while this is challenging work, intrapreneurs take to lean startup methods quite well. They want to launch successful products and they see it as a great tool for solving some of the challenges they have had in the past (e.g. premature scaling of products that aren't sufficiently tested).

Innovation Rhythm

The real challenge is what happens after the training and coaching is done. The newly trained innovators often find themselves in a company that is not set up to support their new skills and ways of working. Intrapreneurship and innovation work at a certain rhythm and pace. This is best represented by the design and test loop – in which innovators identify their assumptions, run experiments and use data to make evidence-based decisions. This rhythm also helps innovators to identify customer needs, build the right solution and find the correct business model.

In contrast, large organisations have a different rhythm based on executing the current business model. This is often the antithesis of the innovator's rhythm: long budget cycles, thirty-page business cases and incentives based on revenue growth. This mismatch is problematic for grassroots movements. As much as innovators try to do their work, they are often stifled by the management processes in their company. Paradoxically, the same leaders who sent the innovators out for lean startup training find themselves telling the same people to 'stop experimenting and write a business case'.

Organisational Design

Lean startup training in itself is just not enough. In order for a lean startup culture to thrive in large companies, we have to transform the rhythm of our management systems to match the rhythm of innovators. Clayton Christensen was right: organisational capabilities trump human capabilities.[10] A bad organisational system will beat

---

10 Christensen, C. M. (2013). *The innovator's dilemma: when new technologies cause great firms to fail.* Harvard Business Review Press.

a well-trained human being every time. The management tools we have in our companies right now have been developed meticulously over decades and centuries. Company leaders have excellent methods to calculate profit and loss, balance sheets, net present value and return on investment.

These tools may be the wrong tools for managing innovation. But what are we bringing to the table as pirates with a similar stature? Nothing.

Management Tools

If innovation is now required as part of doing business, what we need are new tools to manage the process. Within the lean startup movement, we have a great toolbox for innovators to use in their work, including business model canvases to outline the big picture and experiment boards for testing our findings. What we now need to work on most diligently are tools for the leaders who manage innovators. If we have given our innovation teams the best contemporary tools to create breakthrough products, we should not leave our leaders to manage innovation with the traditional tools they have always used.

One key management area that needs new tools is investment decision-making. Traditionally, managers have asked for thirty-page business cases before they can release funding. This long-standing practice should be replaced with innovation accounting – a way to evaluate innovation team progress without the usual metrics. We need to work with our leaders to develop a process in which they ask the right questions at the right time. These questions need to match the rhythm of innovators.

Investment decision-making is just the tip of the iceberg. We also

need to develop similar methods for strategy development and portfolio management. So there is a lot to do in order for innovation to enjoy sustained success in any company. Many intrapreneurs are only interested in the fun and games of sticky notes and whiteboards. But this is not enough. We have to do the hard work of making innovation an integral part of how the organisation is managed.

So you have a choice to make. Do you really want to be a pirate in the navy? What form is this piracy going to take? Are you going to work on transforming your company or focus on making products to create new growth? Can you really choose one and not the other in the first place? Let's see…

Making this one choice will help you focus

Being an intrapreneur is a very difficult job at the best of times. However, it gets even harder when the intrapreneur is not clear what their job actually is. I once had a conversation with an innovation leader from a large retail company that had also launched a bank as a challenger brand. In discussing his struggles within the large company and the choices he faced, we landed on a major decision that he had been avoiding.

Did he view his job as helping his teams launch successful new products in the market? Or did he view his job as leading the transformation of his company into an organisation with a new set of processes and tools that could sustain innovation? Could he realistically do the former without doing the latter? Choices, choices, choices.

As far as I am concerned, making this single choice in an explicit way will help innovators focus on what needs to be done. Understanding the distinction between these two options is critical, even if in the end you make the choice to do both. Are we focusing on creating new products to drive growth, or are we trying to change how our company manages innovation?

Growth versus transformation – that is the choice to make.

Transformation

Transforming your organisation will help innovation thrive in the long term. In *The Corporate Startup*,[11] we recommend building an innovation engine, a set of processes and tools enabling a repeatable process for taking creative ideas and transforming them into profitable business models. To build an innovation engine requires that we change how our company develops innovation strategy, makes investment decisions, measures progress and incentivises intrapreneurs.

Transforming companies is challenging work and it is not for the faint-hearted. But it is also highly rewarding. Creating the right

---

[11] Viki, T., Toma, D., & Gons, E.. (2017). The Corporate Startup. *Deventer: Management Impact.*

environment for innovators can help a company prepare for the future, while running its core business for current success. But if you are a pirate in the navy, the question becomes: Is that your job? If so, then you need to be thinking about how you can do that well.

New Growth

The transformation choice is relatively different from the choice to focus on new growth. While transformation makes innovation easier, it is also possible to innovate in organisations that do not have an innovation ecosystem. This is difficult work that requires the pirate to be politically astute, find diplomats and champions to support their work, and help their teams to make progress.

Ryan Jacoby has written a concise, must-read book entitled *Making Progress*,[12] in which he argues that the first and foremost job of an innovation leader is helping their teams to make progress. This means that they have to define what progress means within their organisation, set a clear innovation agenda, build the right teams and then inspire, support and reward those teams for making progress. According to Jacoby, creating processes and managing transformation is not an innovation leader's job.

The work of leading innovation can result in the creation of a new engine, but this is an incidental side effect. What the innovation leader has to do to make progress – the political landmines they have to avoid, the clever ways they discover to protect their teams and acquire resources – can forge a new path to transform the organisation, while the innovation leader celebrates success. But

---

12   Jacoby, R. (2018). *Making Progress. New York: Sense and Respond Press.*

the transformation of the company is not the leader's goal. It simply happens while they are focused on creating new growth.

Make the Choice

Whatever you do as a pirate in the navy, do not get caught in between focusing on transformation and creating new growth. Make a clear choice. There are risks involved in both approaches and you have to be aware of these. If you focus on new growth, be aware of the corporate antibodies within your organisation and develop ways to avoid them. You have to become an extremely savvy politician.

This book is about transformation. My passion is to help innovators avoid having to run an underground movement inside their company. I believe that an exclusive focus on new growth does not produce new innovation in a consistent way. Instead, what you get are one-off projects that succeed. I also know from experience that transformation takes a long time to produce results. It requires patience, grit and tenacity.

But this book is also about how you can use innovation projects to drive new growth and create a new innovation engine. For example, creating new products that generate new revenue can provide a transformation team with early wins that demonstrate the value of innovation and the new ways of working. Such stories then provide much needed momentum for the long-term transformation project. But we still need to keep the main thing the main thing. A clear focus on transformation can help future intrapreneurs make progress by removing obstacles to innovation.

The choice is yours. Blue pill or red pill? Growth or transformation?

The three human barriers to transformation

We are now going to proceed on the assumption that you have chosen the red pill. You have decided to take on the Matrix and transform your company: a pirate working collaboratively with the navy to help it become innovative. I couldn't think of a better script myself.

But like in all good movies there will be pain and strife along the way to achieving your goal. This is because, while the creation of new products with good business models is hard to achieve, transformation is excruciatingly difficult. A company can only reap the benefits of innovation if we succeed in changing people and their mindsets. This is the human side of transformation and it is the most difficult because it speaks to people's deep-seated needs for stability and an almost instinctive resistance to change.

It is not just about teaching people innovation skills or implementing new management processes. Transformation relates to universal human challenges. Human life is a constant tension between progress and inertia. For most people, changes within their company can feel like chaos is being introduced into their once predictable workplace. On the other hand, people also recognise that things do not stay the same and change is inevitable.

Transformation is most difficult in traditional organisations with a long-running history of success and low employee turnover. It can be a blessing and a curse to have employees who love working at a successful company and strongly identify with it. It is a blessing because these employees understand the fundamental DNA of the company and this can serve as a true north during any transformation program.

However, this employee commitment can become a challenge when people start to confuse their daily rituals and ways of working as the way things will always be. When a transformation is taking place, it forces people to answer a key question: What are the truly essential elements that are the core DNA of our company? And what are the ways of working and technologies that can and must be changed?

While innovators will often focus on their team's plans for transformation and discuss roadmaps for implementation, the human barriers to transformation remain largely unaddressed. So as we begin the road to transformation, we have to discuss the three key human barriers to transformation that have to be dealt with before our program can succeed.

1. *Inertia:* This is the tendency for people to do nothing or remain unchanged. Inertia is particularly strong when things are going well within a company. Unless there is a crisis, most people will question why change within the company is necessary at all. The company is thriving, well-established practices are working and we are making profits. So why do we need to change? Most people cannot sense their business environment changing before it's too late. However, if companies wait until there is a crisis it might too late to transform it effectively. Inertia is something that must be addressed by leaders directly. It has to be communicated to employees that current success is not a guarantee of future success. Leaders must provide clearly articulated reasons for the transformation that paint an aspirational view of the future.

2. *Doubt:* In every organisation, there are people who understand the need for change. Their biggest barrier is doubt. They doubt that such change can ever happen in a company such as theirs. Many of them would have experienced a number of failed innovation programs. So they will take the point of view that the current transformation is just another one of those. I have been in meetings with people who remember how their company tried and failed to innovate several times. They don't believe that their leadership is capable of leading such changes. So they choose to hunker down and get on with their work – this latest change program will soon blow by. Ironically, this is a self-fulfilling prophecy. Transformation can fail to happen because the very people that are supposed to drive it don't believe that change can happen.

3. *Cynicism:* This is the human barrier that can be the most frustrating for pirates in the navy. This is the schadenfreude that some people feel when our transformation program runs into problems or has to change direction. Since they already doubt our work, these people will use any failure or change of plan as an example to illustrate how they always knew that their company's leadership and the innovation team were incompetent. This is frustrating because there is no transformation program that ever runs without problems or challenges. Indeed, our willingness to change and adapt our plans is a good sign that we are listening and testing our ideas. Cynics can be like rotten apples in a transformation program and must be addressed directly.

In a *Forbes* article on digital transformation trends,[13] Daniel Newman noted that company culture is still the biggest barrier to transformation. Beyond planning the roadmap and implementing the processes, we need to think seriously about the human side of transformation. We must never forget that we are dealing with people. We will need their support and engagement to succeed. So we must always begin with a little humility.

---

13   Newman, D. (2018). '2018 digital transformation trends: where are we now?', Forbes: https://www.forbes.com/sites/danielnewman/2018/08/20/2018-digital-transformation-trends-where-are-we-now/#4fe61618c647

Chapter 3
A LITTLE HUMILITY

You are not Elon Musk

Being humble is the hardest thing for a pirate to do. Humility sometimes seems to be the exact opposite of their DNA. In their own minds they are Elon Musk. I have often been shocked by the condescending language I have heard some of them use to describe their colleagues. Their contempt for leaders that 'don't get it' is palpable. You can feel their frustration and righteous anger every time you speak to them.

But I believe that this unabashed self-confidence is problematic. In fact, I can almost predict which innovators are going to flame out in their roles quickly by how much humility they lack. There are already difficult organisational barriers to overcome and adopting an arrogant tone makes things worse. In fact, I have seen some innovators create barriers where none existed just by how they act.

So let's dispense with any myths you may have about yourself. You are not Elon Musk! You are not a hero here to save the company – and you are not working in a company full of idiots. The approach you take within the company will make your attempts at transformation easier or harder.

Innovators have to embrace the reality that nobody owes them their faith or attention. At the beginning of an innovation movement, we just don't have the credibility to insist that our approach is the correct one. What we are seeking is for the company to give us space and permission to try new things and demonstrate our competence as an innovator.

And it really doesn't matter if you have been a successful founder of a startup before. Corporate innovation is a totally different kettle of fish. There are many more political hurdles to overcome inside large companies before a new product can be taken to scale. This is why building good relationships matters.

Acting like you are Steve Jobs or Elon Musk before you have earned the right to behave like a big shot will only earn you enemies. What you don't want early on is people in the company that are emotionally invested in seeing you fail. You want to create the exact opposite of that.

So start with a little humility. If you were Elon Musk you would be running SpaceX. Instead you are likely working in a large company, getting a monthly salary. Enough of the egotistical nonsense. You have to work to build strong relationships within the company to succeed, especially with middle managers.

In defense of middle managers who stifle innovation

There is no group of leaders that innovators find more frustrating than middle managers. Whenever I am in conversations with intrapreneurs about their struggles in large enterprises, they mostly blame middle managers. To their minds, these up-and-coming

A LITTLE HUMILITY

leaders with MBAs are the real problem in getting an innovation culture embedded within the company. Middle managers are on a specific career trajectory and will not do anything to upset the apple cart. Intrapreneurs who report to these managers can find their role really frustrating.

The Permafrost

I have heard middle managers being referred to as *permafrost*: the place where all good ideas go to die. In most companies it often feels as if the top executives get it. These executives always place innovation as a top priority in all their strategic goals and communications. The innovation teams also seem to get it. They have attended lean startup, design thinking and business model-design workshops. They are keen to work on some potentially disruptive new products.

But between these two parts of the company lies the 'permafrost': the managers who are tasked with delivering the top executives' goals by managing the product teams. Clayton Christensen points out that top executives may think that they determine what happens in their companies. But the truth is that their companies are really run by the middle management.[14] It is this strata that can stifle an innovation project before it even gets the attention of top executives.

Misaligned Incentives

But how fair is this characterisation of middle managers? Is it really true that they don't want to work on exciting new products? In my experience, this judgement is wholly unfair. Middle managers are sometimes used as punching bags by top executives. The truth is that most top executives simply talk about how innovation is important for their company. But their private actions can communicate a different message.

Most middle managers are incentivised by their top executives to reach specific revenue and profit numbers. Their ability to deliver on these goals is the only conversation that happens when they meet. Their bonuses and promotions depend on their ability to execute and deliver on the core products, *not* on bringing new innovative products into the pipeline. I have met very few middle managers who include innovation as one of the annual measures of success.

A lot of executives talk through both sides of their mouth. On the one hand they are saying the company needs more innovation, but on the other they are only going to reward execution and revenues on the core products. Most leaders forget that the culture in their

---

14 Christensen, C.M. (1997). The Innovator's Dilemma. *Boston: Harvard Business Review Press.*

companies is determined by what they reward and celebrate. So they can talk about innovation all they want, but unless they start incentivising their middle managers to do so, the culture in their companies won't change.

So what is the middle manager supposed to do when an innovator comes up with a new disruptive product idea? Given how they are being managed from the top, their first question will be how much revenue this new idea will generate for the business this year. This question means that most innovative ideas are dead on arrival. The innovator will walk away from the conversation frustrated and mumbling insults under their breath.

What is happening here is a game of smoke and mirrors. The innovator assumes that they are aligned with the CEO and that the middle manager is simply getting in the way. What they don't realise is that the CEO is in the same boat as the middle managers. They are fighting the same battle with the dominant core business.

The question for pirates in the navy is whether they can find the humility to frame the conversation another way. We should not be asking middle managers to ruin their careers by working with us. Investing in our ideas would create a hole in their budgets and revenues that they then have to explain to the top executives. This is completely unfair. Even if you really are Elon Musk.

To succeed, we have to create a shared understanding with our middle managers and work with them to convince corporate leaders to change how they reward and incentivise innovation. This layer of permafrost will only thaw if middle managers' incentives are aligned with the company's goals for innovation. If we ignore this fact, we will continue to engage in an artificial proxy war and make no progress.

Innovation is management

I have learned that the Steve Jobs most innovators want to be is the glamorous version on stage, presenting the latest iPhone at an Apple event. Not many innovators want to learn how to be Steve Jobs doing the day-to-day innovation grind. There is a tendency to value ideas and creativity over dynamic systematic management processes.

Although I can clash with leaders, I often find myself at loggerheads with innovators. A lot of these folks seem to hate process. They mostly want to be left alone to get on with it. If they engage in any process at all, it's generally with lightweight, easy-to-use tools. They are mostly interested in the 'fun' parts of innovation: brainstorming, ideation and canvases with Post-It notes and sharpies.

It has always struck me as unreasonable that some intrapreneurs expect their progress not to be tracked and managed. They want resources from the company, but they don't want any accountability for their work. If innovation is to become a legitimate part of the business, we have to be more serious about our practices.

It is not a form of humiliation to be held accountable. Also, it does not stifle our creativity. Investments in innovation have to produce returns and executives cannot be expected to keep pouring money into failing projects. This is, of course, not to denigrate the value of vision and ideas. Ideas still lie at the heart of innovation. Without ideas and vision there would be no new products to manage. The choice between vision and management is not a dichotomous either-or. Rather it is an inclusive 'both-and'. Innovation is both inspiration and a systematic process.

The right way to manage innovation is to use incremental investing or metered funding – where specific goals are linked to each round of investment. This investment process involves making small investments, while teams are searching for value propositions and business models that work. As teams show success, they can then get large follow-on investments. The small initial investments allow leaders to learn if the product idea has potential before they make further investments. This is different from making one large investment based on a business plan.

In return for investment, innovators are expected to get out of the building and confirm that there are real customers with needs and problems they will pay to have solved. They also have to validate that the solution they are creating serves those customer needs well. Finally, they have to find a profitable business model with which to deliver value to customers.

These steps on the innovation journey provide our leaders with a way to make investments and track progress. Since the early stages of an innovation journey are mostly about testing the market and potential solutions, small amounts of money can be invested. As ideas start to show traction (e.g. early paying customers), companies can then make larger investments to get to product-market fit and then take the product to scale.

This also means that there is no need for innovators to have contentious relationships with their leaders, managers and colleagues. Innovators can get the resources they need to work on ideas without having to write long business plans. But this investment comes with an expectation that they have to track their work and demonstrate progress before they receive further investment.

The humility to allow ourselves to be held accountable will earn us the credibility to be allowed to begin doing our work. If we are to resist being held accountable, this will create suspicions about our intentions. As pirates in the navy, we want credibility and legitimacy. We are no longer running an underground operation.

Innovation orphans

Earlier I observed how large companies are often unwilling to take successful ideas to scale. Part of the challenge is a lack of leadership or a clear strategy. The other part of the challenge is a lack of humility on the part of the intrapreneurs.

Inside the silo of their lab they generate loads of brilliant ideas. I have even worked with teams that have really great traction with customers for their ideas. But when they want to scale, they cannot find support from executives within their company.

This is a very humbling experience for many innovators. They were expecting to be thanked and celebrated. But alas, no one in the company appreciates their brilliance. They are learning late in the process that they are misaligned with their parent company. If they had managed their relationship with the company better, their brilliant ideas would now not be innovation orphans (i.e. new products and

services that customers want, but your company doesn't want to sell). Below are some best practice guidelines to help intrapreneurs ensure that their ideas don't end up as innovation orphans:

- *Don't create an innovation silo:* This point wades into the debate on whether innovation should be done within the company or in a physically separate innovation lab. But regardless of where innovation happens, the innovation teams must not become siloed away from the parent company. Even if we work in separate innovation labs, we must strive to stay connected to the parent company. We have to work on problems that are of value to the leadership within the company, and we have to work on gaining trust through letting the rest of the company experience and understand our innovation methods.

- *Get strategic alignment:* This ensures that the projects we are working on matter to someone else in the company beyond our innovation team. It is important that innovators work with their executive leadership to define and agree an innovation strategy for the company. This is a clearly stated point of view as to how the company is going to use innovation to respond to key trends. It defines the types of innovation projects the company will invest in and scale. Such clarity at the strategy level makes conversations about successful ideas easier, because innovation teams have been working on projects deemed strategically important from the beginning.

- *Agree on process alignment:* Sychronising innovation processes with company strategy ensures that we have an agreed method for tracking and measuring success. Innovation teams need to work with their leadership to help them understand how to ask the right questions at the right time. For example, during the early stages of a project, the right question to ask is whether there is a real customer need that can be solved by our solution. Asking for revenue projections before we understand what customers want is the wrong question at the wrong time. Process alignment can help innovators manage conversations with their leadership teams as they prepare for scale.

Innovation orphans highlight the fact that innovation cannot succeed in a repeatable way if it is done under the radar. We want to make our piracy a legitimate part of the company. Having successful ideas often requires teams to make themselves heard by the leadership within their company. How those leaders respond to our success will determine whether or not we end up with innovation orphans on our hands. As such, it is important to already be practising humility within our organisation, and working to define strategy and innovation processes before the problem of innovation orphans arises.

So how do we get started? We must begin with the discovery process: we need to learn and understand how our company currently works.

Chapter 4
START WITH DISCOVERY

Fools rush in

A lot of innovators I have met are impatient people. By the time we start working together, they are already fed up with their company. They know something needs to be done and they just want to jump in and get started. So they will take whatever opportunity they get and run with it.

I believe that this is the wrong approach. As much as we are keen to get started, it is also important to ensure that we are working on the right projects. This is a lesson I learned from making many mistakes in my own work. I was often happy to take whatever innovation project the leadership team threw my way. And I have done it all – idea jams, hackathons, startup weekends, training workshops and innovation sprints. It did not matter whether what I was working on was the right thing for the company at that time or not.

'You've got to start somewhere,' I often hear intrapreneurs say. In my opinion, this is true and I couldn't agree more. But it is important to recognise that this statement does not mean 'You've got to start anywhere.' There is a difference.

While you have to start somewhere, it is important that you choose the right place to start. Always remember the main goal. We want to make entrepreneurship a legitimate and respected part of our company. We want the work we do to have a lasting impact. We are trying to create a repeatable innovation process. This is why we can't just start anywhere by doing random activities.

We have to first develop a deep understanding of our company. We have to come to grips with the context in which we will be operating. Ultimately, we will have to do the hard work needed to put in place the right internal structures, processes and environment. Therefore, the first question for us to answer is: How ready is our company to support and nurture innovation?

Is your company ready for innovation?

This is a question I have hardly ever heard asked by pirates in the navy. Even worse, very few intrapreneurs can give you clear answers as to what 'innovation readiness' looks like. They have no frameworks for assessing whether or not their company is ready to support innovation. There are three main elements that pirates in the navy need to think about before they start working: leadership support, organisational design and innovation practice.[15]

Leadership Support

Without explicit and visible support from our leadership, most innovation programs are dead on arrival. Leadership support needs to go beyond just words that encourage innovation to doing the following:

- *Strategic guidance:* Leaders must provide innovation teams with an innovation strategy that makes explicit where they should focus their efforts. This strategic guidance must be clear or known by most people within the organisation.

---

15 Developed in 2019 by Strategyzer's Alex Osterwalder, Yves Pigneur and Tendayi Viki. Innovation Readiness Assessment. Strategyzer: https://blog.strategyzer.com/posts/innovation-readiness-assessment-tool

 LEADERSHIP SUPPORT
 STRATEGIC GUIDANCE
 RESSOURCE ALLOCATION
 PORTFOLIO MANAGEMENT

 ORGANISATIONAL DESIGN · LEGITIMACY POWER · BRIDGE TO THE CORE ·  REWARDS INCENTIVES

 INNOVATION PRACTICE ·  INNOVATION TOOLS ·  PROCESS MANAGEMENT ·  SKILLS DEVELOPMENT

- *Resource allocation:* In a lot of companies, there are no official resources for innovation. Instead, intrapreneurs have to hustle and scrape for resources that can be pulled from them at any moment. Leaders need to make sure that they are allocating budget, time and resources that are protected from encroachment by the core business.

- *Portfolio management:* Innovation cannot flourish if the leadership are exclusively focused on running and improving their core business. Instead, leaders need to be actively involved in making investments to explore future opportunities for growth.

Organisational Design

Beyond leadership, we also need to design our company structures to support innovation. As intrapreneurs, we have to build enablers and remove blockers for innovation practice to flourish:

- *Legitimacy and power:* If innovation teams have to constantly fight for their right to exist, then innovation has little legitimacy or power within your company. While being a pirate might be fun, innovation is more sustainable when it is an explicit part of our institutional structures.

- *Bridge to the core:* It is often difficult for innovation teams and the core business to collaborate. In fact, there can be conflict for resources, which the core business inevitably wins. As such, we need clear policies that help innovation teams collaborate with the core business.

- *Rewards and incentives:* Most companies manage innovation using the same reward and incentive systems as the core business. The annual targets and review process for bonuses makes it difficult to celebrate failure. Innovation needs to have a dedicated and different incentive system.

Innovation Practice

Innovation cannot be done using the same tools and practices that we use within the core business. Planning and executing are not the right processes for innovation. Instead, innovators need to iterate to design and test their ideas:

- *Innovation tools:* Companies need to adopt the right tools for designing business models and testing assumptions. Adopting tools from agile software development, a new business model, lean startup and design thinking will help facilitate the innovation process. These tools need company-wide adoption, rather than adoption in small pockets of the company.

- *Process management:* As already noted, innovation teams need to adopt iterative methods for testing and reducing risk. In line with this best practice, our processes for managing innovation should be optimised to systematically track and measure how well teams are reducing the level of risk in new ideas.

- *Skills development:* It is a myth that entrepreneurship cannot be learned. It is possible to develop and train innovation skills within our teams. Beyond training, we also need to give people the experience of working on and running innovation projects. Such skills training should be provided across the whole organisation, including people in departments such as HR and finance.

Innovation Readiness

So before launching our innovation projects, we have to discover the lie of the land. We have to find out how ready the company is to support innovation. We can only do this via the process of discovery. So before we start planting the flowers of great new ideas, we need to find out whether our corporate garden is fertile with the right nutrients to nurture innovation.

Learn from those that tried before you

As much as you think you are a corporate hero in the making – you are not. I have already reminded you that you are not Elon Musk. You are probably not the first person in your company ever to try to innovate – so you are not a pioneer. If you look around hard enough, you will find others who have tried before you.

Some have had some limited success and others have failed. You may not be able to see the scars of the knives in their backs as evidence to prove it. So if you want to succeed, you need to take the time to learn from these people. Approach them without judgement and treat them with respect.

What I always find interesting about companies is their frequent ability to recycle staff and not fire them for failed innovation projects. While this is a strange practice for the company, for you it's a treasure trove of information. It means that there are people still around in the company, probably now working in different roles, that you can mine for information. So use your internal networks to find these people and ask for their help and support.

But tread carefully here; these people are not losers who did not know what they were doing. They may feel fragile and defensive but with the right approach, they will open and share with you the mistakes they made and the lessons they learned. Their assistance will be invaluable to you in so many ways – the landmines that tripped these people up are still in the company and these people will know exactly where they are.

Remember, companies have a way of breaking intrapreneurs and humbling them – these people are pioneers, they may just need reminding of that fact to reignite their enthusiasm and commitment to innovation. So don't look down on them or dismiss their previous efforts.

View them as early reconnaissance teams that laid the groundwork for future innovators – and what they learned on their journey is gold dust. Humbly communicate with them that you need their help to learn and fully understand what (or who) to avoid within the organisation.

For example, they can help you to find answers to the following questions:

- Where are all the corporate traps and bureaucracy?
- Which stakeholders are the most difficult? Which ones are most supportive?
- Are there any other early adopters of innovation within the company who you might target and work with?

Do not limit your conversations to only those innovators that remain in the company. Learn what you can about the people who tried to innovate, were knocked back and left the company. Is there anybody still in touch with them or who knows where they are now? Can they give you names or introduce you so that you can meet them and learn from their experiences too? Invite these former employees for coffee or a drink so that you can have a chat and pick their brains.

This is not wasted effort on your part. In my experience it will save you from making the same mistakes that these pioneers made. So, embrace this truth – you are NOT that special. If you want to be successful, first park your ego. Even if the CEO loves you and your wonderful ideas, you will have to build other strong and sustainable relationships in order to succeed within the company. Talking to those that came before you will help with this.

Map all activity happening

Here is another interesting and possibly surprising fact for you – your program is probably not the only activity centred around innovation that is happening inside your company at the moment. Organisations have a way of spawning a lot of random innovation projects – all claiming to do the same things and all with different or even competing objectives. A little unsettling, isn't it?

In some large companies I have worked with, innovators are constantly running into each other. They are asking for the same resources, building similar products and even talking to the same customers. There is so much competition and duplication of effort, which is a great waste of time and talent.

This burst of innovative activity has become a real problem since innovation theatre made innovation a sexy thing to do within companies. Now everyone wants to be recognised as an innovative rock star in the making.

Don't join in on this waste of time. Don't be one of those pirates who just wants to get started and is willing to do anything to get their piece of the pie. Always be thinking about how you can create value for your company using innovation. So take some time to find out exactly what is going on, who's doing what and where. This will ensure that your own efforts aren't either crushed, diluted or even obliterated in this project mishmash.

You will soon discover that these innovation activities sit at different layers within the company from top to bottom. Leaders within various divisions and departments will often kick off their own programs without paying much attention to what else is happening in the company. This is your chance to make great connections.

For your efforts at transforming the company, to succeed you have to develop a good understanding of these initiatives and their goals. So, just as you connected with those who tried and failed, you now need to talk to those people running current innovation programs to learn:

- Why were the programs set up? What are they trying to achieve?
- Are these programs focused on creating new growth, transforming the company or both? How much impact are they actually having on either creating new growth or transforming the company?
- What challenges are they facing? What are the main enablers and blockers within the company?

Once you have all the answers you need, you can then take the time to map all the innovation activity taking place within your company. To do this, I have developed the 'Innovation Activity Map'. On the vertical axis, you can score each activity in terms of its potential to create new growth. On the horizontal axis, you can score each activity in terms of its potential to create a new innovation engine and transform your company. This tool can be used to map all the innovation projects being currently undertaken within your company.

After mapping all the innovation activities you will be able to identify gaps and opportunities for you to make a meaningful and sustainable contribution. If you take a closer look it will be possible for

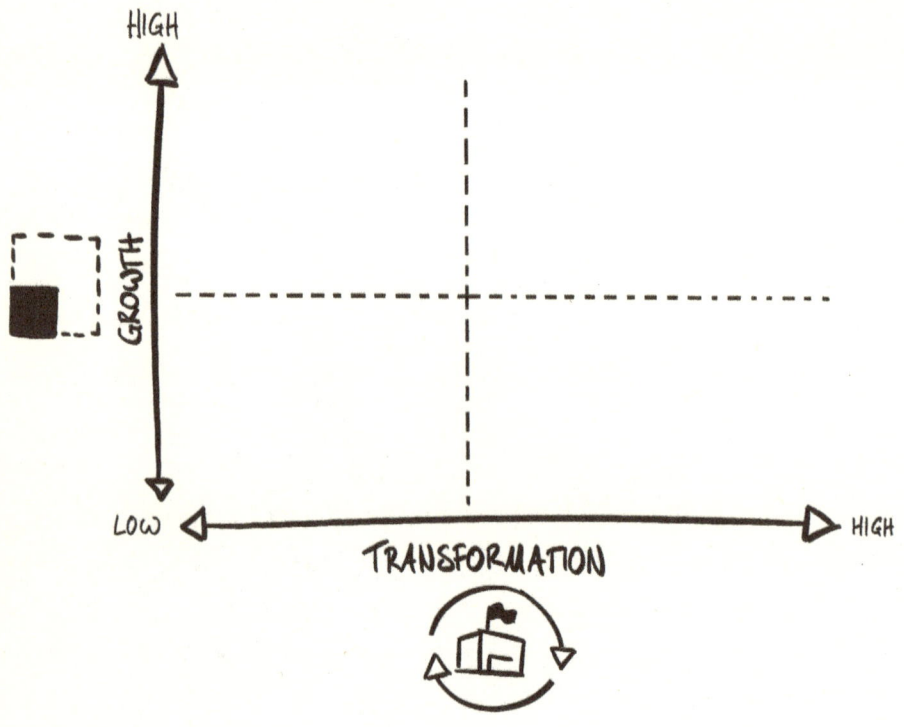

you to form alliances. In other instances, there will be great programs that simply need to be supported by your efforts.

The more politically problematic projects will be those that score low on both growth and transformation. Do not tackle these with a view to shutting them down at the moment. This is not a good time to make enemies. Instead, find ways to work with them to help improve on what they are doing. And if this can't be done, just ignore these programs for the time being. At least now you know who is running them and what they are working on.

Understanding what is happening inside your company is important. The people running these programs can become your allies, or enemies who can trip you up, depending on your approach and how you conduct yourself. You will never be able to win all of them over but I can guarantee that with the right approach you will earn the support of enough allies to create a strong movement.

Talk to all stakeholders

Sometimes, innovation programs are fortunate enough to begin their life out of the shadows and get launched with great fanfare. These are the lucky few pirates who are embraced by the CEO speaking highly of their innovation team and how they are going to transform the fortunes of the company. You may be one of them and perhaps your own work was launched in this way.

So, you're flying high and basking in the love of your CEO. But stop right there and take a breath – you might be in desperate need of a reality check. Sure, the CEO loves you and sure, your program is looking really good right now, but you need to understand that while this is necessary support, it is not enough for you to succeed. It is probably less than 10 per cent of what you will need to succeed.

Now you've crashed back down to earth and your feet are firmly on the ground, you may be ready to hear that you've got a lot more work to do to convince other stakeholders of your value. When innovators feel that they have the support of the CEO, they think that they can do whatever they want and ignore other stakeholders within the business. This is a huge mistake.

Earlier I spoke out in defence of middle managers who stifle innovation – part of your discovery work is to understand why that happens. Believe it or not, the CEO may be the boss, but they don't run the company. It is the middle managers who make a lot of the daily decisions. The decision these people make can either help or hinder your work. Rather than just treating them as ignoramuses who don't understand innovation, take the time to understand their motivations.

Middle of Nowhere

Some stakeholders stifle innovation because they just don't get it. They don't see its role within the company. These are the really difficult ones to deal with. We have to approach them with caution. Other stakeholders see innovation as important but don't believe that it is their job to deal with it. For the stakeholders that don't believe innovation is their job, education and persuasion may be more appropriate.

Other stakeholders stifle innovation because of how the company incentivises their work. These stakeholders get it and would love to support innovation. The problem is that the leadership in your company only incentivises and rewards their performance on the core business.

So while the CEO is publicly loving your work, she is also damaging its impact by only incentivising her middle management teams on the basis of their performance on core products. Other stakeholders don't need to hear you preach to them about the value of innovation. Some already get it. Instead, they need you to work with them at the organisational design layer to change the reward and incentive systems.

So What Do I Do Now?

As a pirate in the navy, it's time to use your head. There are many different ways to work with stakeholders. So before you go off in different directions and start doing work at random, you first have to figure out what is driving any resistant behaviour.

- Is it a lack of understanding?
- Are they really against innovation?
- Or is the organisational design and structure getting in the way?

Critically for you, it is important to acknowledge that stakeholders are not just those who are normally viewed as part of the innovation process (e.g. product managers, heads of divisions or heads of R&D). There are stakeholders in the so-called enabling functions too, such as finance, legal, compliance, branding and HR. In fact, these stakeholders are often much more fundamental to success. So you need to work with them as well.

Remember, the goal is to make innovation a legitimate part of the company. So if you haven't done so already, start building relationships with key stakeholders in your company. These are key allies – you won't get far without them.

Keeping it real

Nobody wants to work with a know-it-all who thinks they are going to save the company. These people are actually very annoying. Some of the most challenging characters I have met are former startup founders who sold their last company and are now moonlighting as corporate innovators. These people may completely ignore key stakeholders or treat them like something stuck to their shoes.

What they fail to realise is that a lot of middle managers are quite adept at quietly frustrating innovation efforts. In fact, they have years of experience doing this. They have been in the company for a while and have many high-level connections. So once the word goes around that you are a jerk, it's over for you.

Let's face it – the only way to really connect with people and get them on board is to leave your ego at the door. So as you conduct your discovery process, keep the following things in mind:

- *Listen carefully:* You have to look at this whole discovery journey as not only a process of learning but also a process of building future alliances, so listen to what is being said and not just what you want to hear.

- *Keep an open mind:* It is very important to not let your own biases influence what you are prepared to learn along the way and the changes you may have to make. There is no value in discovery if you ignore the lessons you could be learning and just press on with the original plan.

- *Authenticity is the key*: At the end of the journey, make a thorough and honest review of what you have learned and use that to decide your next steps in the process.

A key thing I tell innovators who are working on discovery is to keep an eye out for early adopters. Don't overlook them, as these are leaders and managers who get it and want to work using lean startup tools but have not had a chance to do it within their company. Recognise them as fellow pirates in the navy who you can take with you into the next stage of your journey. As Henry Ford once said 'Coming together is a beginning. Keeping together is progress. Working together is success.'

Chapter 5
START SMALL

Resist the urge of the big bang

After doing the discovery work you may start to feel overwhelmed. You will have discovered that there is a lot to do inside your company. A lot more to do than you first assumed. You will have learned that your company does not have a clear innovation strategy. Neither does it have a well-managed innovation process. Investment decisions in innovation are still made using traditional business plans and teams are managed to execute these plans without changing them.

In terms of skills, there will likely be a deficit in knowledge and practical experience within your company. Innovation teams will be using the wrong innovation tools. Or they will be using the right innovation tools but not using them the right way. There will be sticky notes, bean bags, hackathons and idea jams – but no profitable new business models being designed or launched.

At the organisational level, you will have found a company that is not designed to support innovation. There will be misalignments with finance, operations, HR, legal, branding and other key departments.

The discovery work will reveal that you have many layers to influence and change. And if you are beginning your work without the support of the CEO and his executive team, you will have a mountain to climb.

In other words, there will be a lot to do. So, so, so much to do.

When faced with this reality, I have found that innovators either run to their labs and hide or they try to be too ambitious. For now I want to focus on the impatient intrapreneurs that want to see their company change straight away. They are the ones that are most likely to choose a big bang approach.

I have worked with intrapreneurs that try to do everything at the same time. They try to launch new products in multiple divisions, change the hearts and minds of leaders, host a ton of events and run workshops to train everyone in innovation skills. Intrapreneurs that work in this way are the most stressed-out people I have ever met. They are spread too thin and are having little impact on their company. After all, if everything is a priority then nothing is a priority.

Take a Long View

When you took the red pill, I forgot to tell you that transforming a company is a long-term project. You will not be able to do this in a year. It is likely to take you three years if you are a world-class innovator and five years if you are a good innovator. If you are an average innovator, don't even get started – it will take you forever. It takes time to design and implement the right structures, processes and capabilities for innovation. So you will need to be patient.

This long-term nature of the work means that you have to begin by doing the things that have impact. In order to survive a long-term project you need to have early wins in order to build credibility. The initial choices you make must be designed to earn you the goodwill you need within the company to be allowed to get to the next series of steps in your transformation project. You have to start small, and spread your early success stories throughout the organisation. This is the only way to ensure that your work is sustainable in the long term.

Resist the lure of the long-term plan

One of the biggest arguments I have had with innovators is when I try to stop them from developing detailed plans and roadmaps for their transformation projects at this early stage. Although they hate business plans, they still can't resist the lure of the Gantt chart. I have worked with innovation teams that make long-term plans early. These plans are made with details and roadmaps that outline an implementation timeline. What these teams hate the most is when I tell them that none of what they have on their roadmap will happen as they expect.

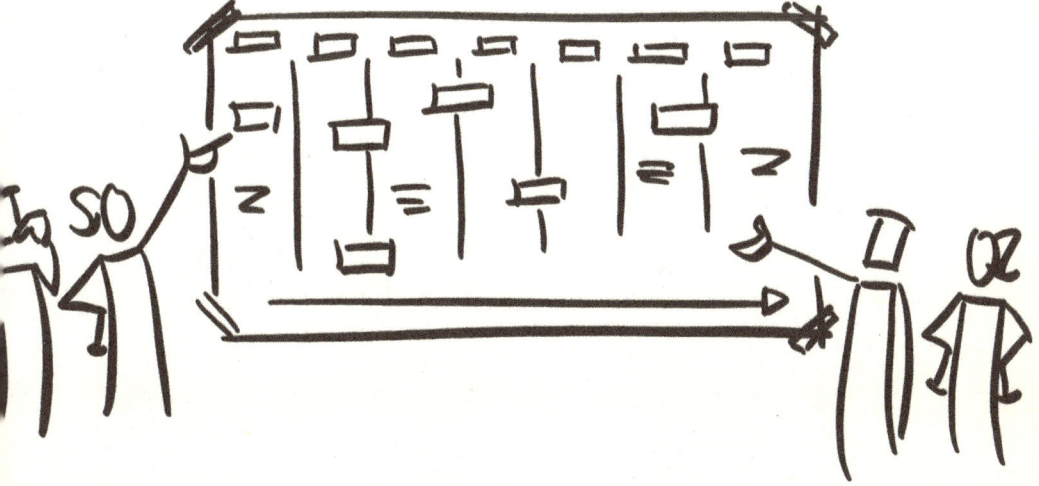

Here is what I have learned from experience: as much as we treat our companies as if they are mechanical structures and processes, they are actually organic, living things. Companies are ultimately made up of the people that work there and the decisions those people make. Believe it or not, these people will not automatically bend to your will. They will respond to your interventions in unexpected ways.

Even if you have CEO and executive level support, the company may still refuse to bend to your will. Only this time the resistance will be quiet. In every company, there are employees that are very good at seeing off transformation programs by frustrating them. So we need to be aware of this challenge as we begin our work.

But even those individuals with good intentions may not necessarily work with us in a way that conforms to our expectations. In one situation I was involved in, our best-laid plans fell apart when we sent out our first emails to the in-house colleagues we wanted to work with. Many of these people got back saying that they wanted to work with us, but due to some pressing deadlines they could only engage with us at a time much later than we were expecting.

This should not have been surprising to our team. It is not like the people in our company were sitting around waiting for our transformation project to begin. They had jobs to do. To paraphrase Steve Blank, even the best-laid transformation plans will not survive their first contact with the organisation. You will need to work in a way that allows you the flexibility to respond to the unexpected. This is not the time to make long-term plans. This is the time to identify early adopters and start working with them. When you start small, you limit the number of moving pieces and this allows you to learn about what works.

Ignore your detractors

One thing you will also have learned during discovery is that not everyone is enthusiastic about innovation. In fact, you will find some leaders and managers who are highly negative and critical. Some will just have a gloomy perception of the company's ability to innovate, while others will be strongly convinced that innovation is not a necessary process for the company. How you respond to this negativity will determine the success of your transformation project.

The human mind is highly tuned to respond to negative stimuli. Bad news travels faster than good news. Research on loss aversion shows that the positive bounce from good news is not as high as the negative dip from bad news.[16] This is why people are advised not to look at the value of their shares on the stock market on a daily basis. They will feel really low on a down day and the positive uplift on a good day will not compensate for those negative feelings.

In life, people tend to pay more attention to their detractors than they do to their supporters. This is important for survival. Identifying an enemy was once a life and death issue. While this might be a great instinct for surviving out in the real world, it is not healthy for an innovation transformation program. We do want to know where we might face challenges within the company, but we don't want to make our detractors the total focus of our work.

I have worked with two types of intrapreneurs, both of whom were overly focused on their detractors. However, they take different approaches to cope with this challenge. As noted earlier, the most

---

16 Kahneman, D. & Tversky, A. (1979). 'Prospect theory: an analysis of decision under risk', *Econometrica 47*: 263–291.

common response is to run and hide in an innovation lab. Then there are the crazy ones who pick a fight with their detractors in the hope of convincing or defeating them. Some have metaphorical scars on their forehead from banging their heads against the wall.

Both these strategies don't work from a transformation perspective. In the first strategy, you are hiding away from the company so you will have limited impact. In the second strategy, you have picked a direct fight with the corporate machine. In my whole career I have never met an innovator who has won that fight. It is career suicide to even try this.

There is a better way to turn detractors into allies: show them the value you are able to create for the company. The only way to show this value is to work closely with people within the company who are on your side at the moment (i.e. early adopters).

Start with early adopters

The presence of detractors within the company can make intrapreneurship feel like a lonely pursuit. However, this feeling is totally misguided. In every large company I have worked with there

are people that want to innovate at every level. There are product teams that are eager to use lean startup methods. There are also leaders who get it and are looking for allies to work with to drive innovation within the company.

These people are your early adopters.[17] They are the ones that will work with you while you develop your approach. They will tolerate your mistakes and root for your success. But how do you find them? Within the lean startup process, an early adopter is defined as a customer who has a problem, is aware of having that problem, has

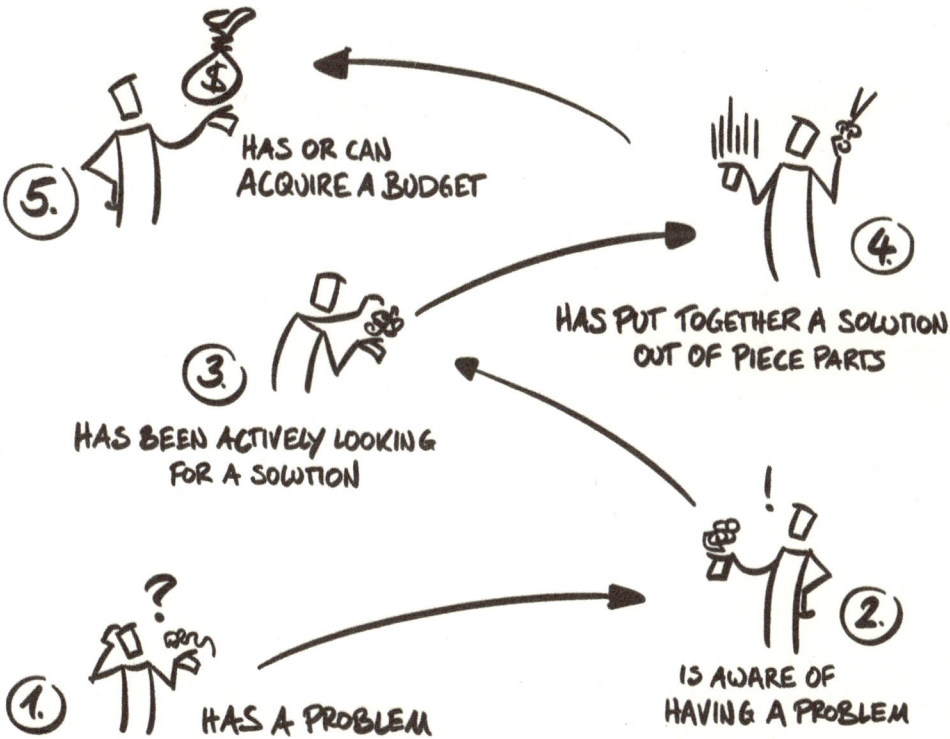

---

17 Adapted from Moore, G. A. (1999). Crossing the chasm: Marketing and selling high-tech products to mainstream customers. *New York, HarperBusiness.*

been actively looking for a solution, has tried to piece together a solution themselves and has or can acquire a budget.[18]

The same principles apply to your search for early adopters within your company. The majority of the work I have done has been commissioned by leaders who:

1. Understand that the world is changing and their company is not well suited to adapt to emerging trends.

2. Are acutely aware that their company has a deficit in the innovation capability needed to survive in the future.

3. Have been actively looking for solutions – which is partly why they have reached out to me.

4. Before they started talking to me, had already sponsored some internal innovation activities (e.g. hackathons or idea competitions).

5. Have the resources to invest and are prepared to make a time commitment to innovation.

Leaders and teams with these five characteristics are the ones you are looking to start working with, not the detractors. These people are your allies – and you don't have to do the hard work of convincing them. One of the goals of the discovery process that you engaged in

---

18 Blank, S., & Dorf, B. (2012). *The startup owner's manual: The step-by-step guide for building a great company. California, KS Ranch*

earlier was to find these early adopters within the company and start working with them.

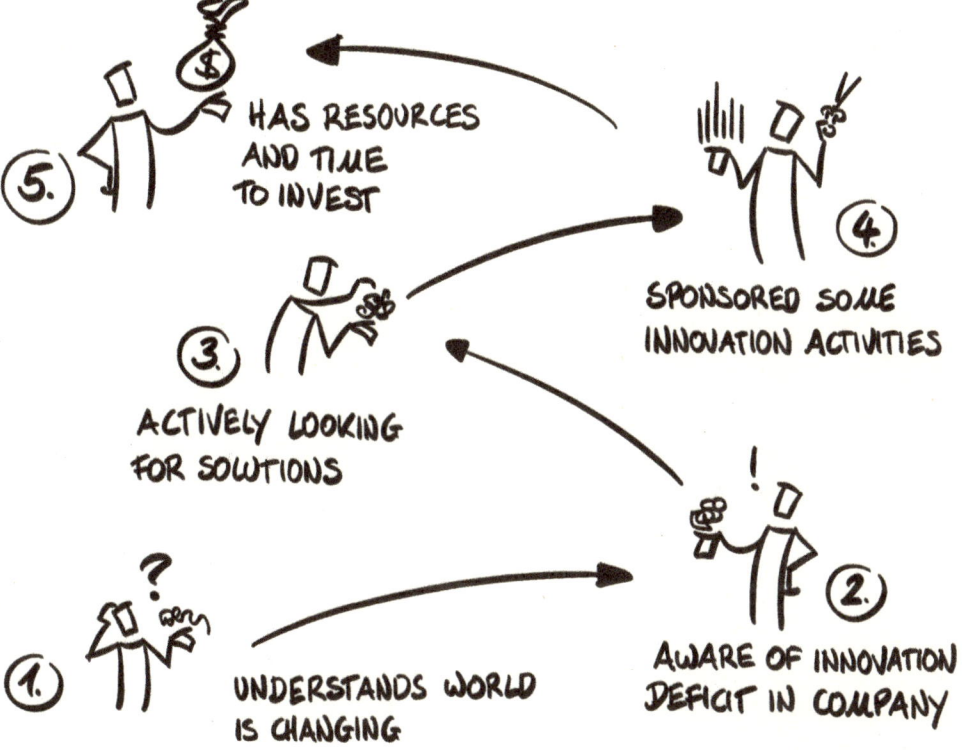

Working with early adopters is great for several reasons. First, it allows you to move fast early because you don't have to do a lot of selling. These people are likely to be super keen to work with you. Second, it allows you to test your innovation tools and methods in a safe space, to make mistakes and learn with people who are not looking to tear you down. Finally, the biggest benefit of working with early adopters is that it can enable you to secure some early wins.

Use minimum viable toolbox

We can work with early adopters to start testing our innovation tools and find out what works within our company. If our goal is to make innovation a repeatable process, we have to start thinking early on about the toolbox we want to have in place. From our perspective, the right innovation tools should cover the spectrum from leadership support to organisational design and innovation practice.

At the leadership support level, there are tools that help with innovation strategy design, portfolio management and investment decision-making. At the organisational design level, we can design processes and tools to help with legitimacy, incentives and building a bridge to the core business.

At the innovation practice level, there are tools that will help you to establish value proposition and business model design, how to prioritise your hypotheses and assumptions about the company, test and iterate, produce innovation metrics and track progress with the right questions.

Very few organisations have all these things in place on day one. So there will be a lot for us to do. But at this early stage, we cannot do everything – nor do we want to. We want to choose elements within the innovation toolbox that are most useful for working with early adopters. As we will discuss next, our goal is to get an early win. As such, we want to minimise friction and get started as soon as we can.

With that in mind, it might be too early to work on strategy design and incentives at the moment. In fact, most of the tools involved in leadership support and organisational design can be safely ignored for the time being. What we can do is begin with our innovation team and use the right tools to get our early win.

As we work with our early adopters, let's use that opportunity to start embedding value proposition and business model design tools. Let's also apply all the tools related to testing ideas, running experiments and making decisions. Our goal is to show that lean innovation tools can work with our company.

For our minimum viable toolbox, I would recommend the following Strategyzer tools for innovation teams:

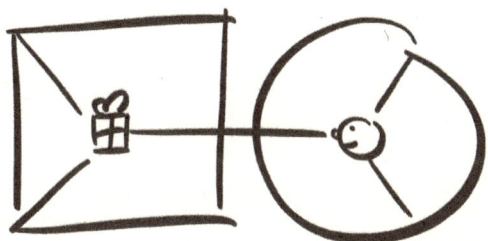

- *Value Proposition Canvas:* This tool allows teams to map their value proposition. It focuses on customer jobs-to-be-done (e.g. get a promotion), the pains they face (e.g. difficult boss) and the gain they are trying to create (e.g. salary increase). It orients innovators towards thinking about how their product or service helps customers with their jobs-to-be-done by reducing pains or creating gains.

- *Business Model Canvas:* This tool allows teams to go beyond the value proposition and consider the business model. It orients innovators towards thinking about how they are going to create and deliver value to customers. It also helps innovators think about how they will get value back from customers and the potential profitability of their business model.

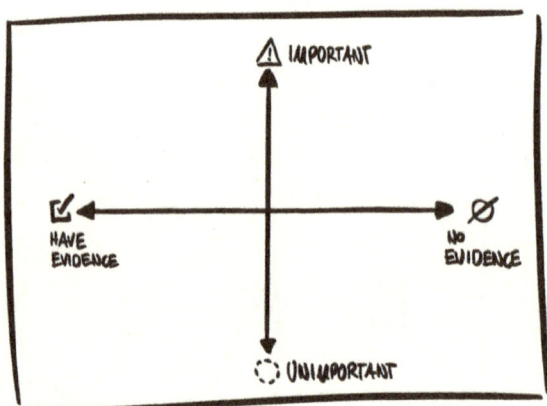

- *Assumptions Prioritisation Map:* Every new business model has untested assumptions (e.g. about customers and their needs). So when we begin working on our projects we want to identify these assumptions and make them explicit. The assumptions can range from whether customers want our product, whether we have the right capabilities to create the product, the right price point for profitability and whether the timing is right to launch our product. After identifying our assumptions, we can then use the prioritisation map to identify the assumptions that are most critical for our business model to succeed and start working on those first.
- *Test and Learning Cards:* These tools allow innovators to design and run experiments to test their ideas. The Test Card can be used to make explicit our assumptions, what we will do to test the assumption, what we will measure and how we will know we

START SMALL

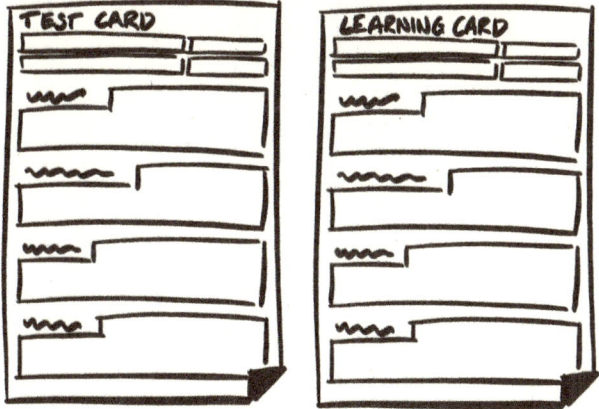

are right. The Learning Card can be used after we have run our experiments to make explicit what we learned and what we plan to do next.

These tools should be enough to get you started. Later in the process you can create a much more comprehensive toolbox that includes portfolio management, innovation accounting and an innovation practice playbook. For the time being, we are looking to start working with basic tools that allow us to make progress. We are aiming to apply these tools to our early adopters' projects and get an early win.

Get early wins

A key part of changing hearts and minds is talking to people. But talk without action is cheap. The trouble with most intrapreneurs I have met is that they can't stop pontificating. They believe so strongly in what they plan to do that they want to talk about it endlessly. The problem is that they are talking about what they plan to do, rather than actually doing it.

I have worked in teams that spend hours designing the best-looking PowerPoint slides. Then they go on a sort of 'political campaign' of talks and meetings with stakeholders. During one such 'campaign' a sceptical stakeholder remarked that our team must not have much to do because we had apparently invested a lot of time in our beautiful slide-deck presentation. Ouch! What I have learned is that while it is important to have conversations, it's even better to do the work.

When innovators don't do the work, stakeholders can ask them a few questions that can stymie their efforts at persuasion:

- Where have you seen this work?
- Have you ever done this type of work yourself?
- Where have you seen this work inside our company?
- Have you ever done this type of work yourself inside our company?

For the first two, intrapreneurs can generally come up with answers from their own experience and by observing other companies like Amazon. Those last two are the killer questions because they haven't done the work inside their own company. So it's time to stop talking endlessly about innovation. Let's start doing it. This is the point of working with early adopters.

To achieve early wins, we need to have the discipline to park our own ambitions as innovators for a period of time. We might have grand visions about the cool things we want to do. However, we won't get the space to do those things until we build credibility and

START SMALL

a reputation for innovation within the company. So our focus should be on helping our early adopters – leaders and business divisions – succeed at whatever they are working on.

When we meet with our early adopters, our goal should not be to sell them our vision of the future. Instead, we should ask them about the challenges they are facing with their innovation projects and how can we help them succeed? These need not be the coolest transformational or disruptive innovation projects. We should be happy, at this stage, to work on incremental or adjacent innovation projects. In fact, we should volunteer to take on the projects that might have stalled and the business is struggling with.

In a *Harvard Business Review* article,[19] Ran Merkazy from Samsung argues that innovators should not push for disruptive ideas too soon. Before they can do that, they need to move the needle by making other people in the organisation believe in them. Merkazy gives an example of one Samsung team that delivered a new, low-risk innovation project to a senior manager in Korea. This manager needed to present new ideas to his own boss. This was good for the

---

19 Wedell-Wedellsborg, T. & Miller, P. (2014). 'How Samsung gets innovations to market'. *Harvard Business Review*: https://hbr.org/2014/05/how-samsung-gets-innovations-to-market

team because he was eventually promoted and became a useful supporter for the team in their more disruptive work.

Our goal in working with early adopters is to show that lean innovation methods work really well within the context of our company. We should view incremental innovation projects as a gift to us. These types of projects have lower levels of risk and are therefore more likely to succeed. What we are looking for are success stories to share with our organisation. And if we succeed like the Samsung team in solving a few headaches for our leaders, we will earn their respect and support.

When we work on these projects with early adopters, our focus should be 100 per cent. We should not get distracted by 'more interesting' projects within the company. There is nothing more annoying to leaders than a flaky innovator who is constantly distracted by the latest cutting-edge ideas. We want to show that we are not just dreamers. We want to show that we can execute innovation all the way to a successful launch, and create revenues and profits.

In order to work with our early adopter leaders and business divisions, we need to set the following conditions:

1. The work will be done using lean innovation methods and tools from the minimum viable toolbox we have put together.

2. The early adopters have to commit people, time and protected resources to make the chosen project a success.

3. We will agree early on the success criteria for the innovation project and how to measure these.

4. We will keep a record of all the work we have done, including assumptions tested, experiments run, lessons learned, pivots made and eventual success.

5. We will be allowed to share the story of this work throughout the organisation as an example of lean innovation practice within the company.

Beyond these conditions, it is up to the leaders and business divisions to choose the projects they want to work on. Our job will be to help drive these projects to success. And when we get that early win, celebrate like crazy – in public.

Celebrate like crazy

The reason we worked with early adopters was to get early wins. The reason we wanted to get early wins was to use them as stories to drive our transformation project. Before we had a win, we had little credibility inside the company. Although many people find very little to disagree with when it comes to the concepts of innovation, their main concern is how to get it done within their company and whether you are the right person or team to do it with.

They are right to be concerned. Not only have they seen many innovation projects go up in flames inside the organisation, they have also seen many so-called pirates do a lot of talking but produce no tangible results. I was once asked by a senior leader after one of my presentations, 'What makes you different from all the other consultants who have come through here saying the same things?'

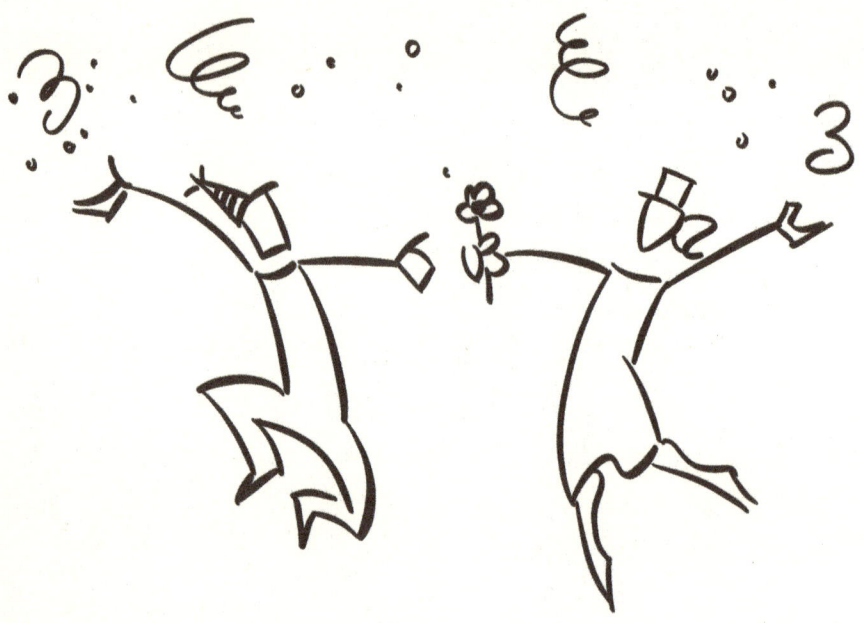

That question stopped me dead in my tracks. I wasn't expecting it, so I didn't have a good response prepared. I just fumbled through something about metrics and tracking progress. I felt fortunate that they chose to work with me after that. But when I thought about it later, it made me understand why many leaders and teams take a wait-and-see approach. They have been down this road already with other innovators. Once bitten, twice shy.

Perceived Norms – Perceived Control
Social science research on behavioural change has found that attitudes alone are not enough to predict behaviour.[20] People may have positive attitudes towards a certain behaviour but fail to react as

---

20 Ajzen, I and Fishbein, M. (1980). Understanding attitudes and predicting social behavior, *Englewood-Cliffs, NJ: Prentice-Hall.*

we expect. This is because there are two other factors that influence whether they act in line with their attitudes: subjective norms and perceived behavioural control.

Subjective norms refer to people's perceptions of the social pressure to perform or not perform a particular behaviour. Perceived behavioural control refers to people's perceptions of how easy it is to perform a particular behaviour. In large organisations, these two factors can have an impact on intrapreneurship. In the first instance, people may perceive that there is social pressure not to act entrepreneurial within their own organisation. And in the second, after seeing intrapreneurs struggle to get things done, they may also perceive that it is not easy to be innovative inside the company.

Getting an early win breaks these perceptions. As we celebrate our success, we provide people with a sense that intrapreneurship is acceptable behaviour within our company. We also show people that innovation can be done within our company. After all, it is their peers whose story we are celebrating.

The Power of Storytelling

Storytelling is a powerful tool, especially when the stories are told by our peers – people like us. By its very nature, innovation is a complex process. If we have abstract conversations with people about it, we will face resistance from naysayers. But stories are disarming. Not only do they aid understanding, they make new concepts tangible and engaging.

This is why we have to go out and tell the stories of the excitement of an innovation project generated inside the company. The ups, the downs and eventual success. This can be really engaging. I have seen the spark in people's eyes when you tell them these stories. It is all the more meaningful to the listeners because it has happened in the context in which they work.

So now we can begin our 'political campaign'. Before, we just had a slide-deck presentation of concepts and external examples. Now we have authentic stories to tell. Let's celebrate these stories like crazy. Make sure you involve your early adopters themselves to tell the stories. This will give us more credibility via peer influence and also give the early adopter leader a chance to shine. When they see other people getting recognition for innovation, others will be motivated to step up and get involved. Before you know it, you have the beginnings of a movement.

In one large company I worked with we did a few things to tell early adopter stories:

- Recording video testimonials
- Writing case studies
- Having early adopters write blog posts
- Featuring success stories in the innovation playbooks
- Having early adopters speak at company workshops

Don't get distracted

After getting an early win, celebrate to the max but don't get distracted. You may now be a local hero inside the company. You may be getting asked to give presentations to leaders about your success and the lessons learned. You might be invited to lunch meetings, to be a judge at hackathons and write articles on the company blog.

Depending on the magnitude of your success, you may even be getting press and media attention.

In the glow of adulation from your new-found fans, it can be easy for you to think you have made it. Before this moment, you were a pariah – nobody wanted to be associated with your plans. Now everybody knows your name. But let's just pump the brakes for a minute. We haven't succeeded yet. We have had some limited success but we still have a long way to go.

Don't forget who you are. You are still a pirate in the navy. The reason you are telling the story of your early wins is to gain credibility in your company so you can go to the next stage. You are not doing it to become famous. Remember to always keep your eye on the prize.

In fact, all the adulation you are currently getting has just put a bigger bullseye on your back for the naysayers. If you think your work on innovation was viewed as an annoyance before, now that you are succeeding you are viewed as a genuine threat. So humility and focus are needed more than ever. You may have won over a few more people to your cause, but there is still a lot to do.

In fact, your early win can be rightly viewed as another innovation in a series of one-off projects. This is not very different to what was happening before you started. Remember, our goal is to make innovation a repeatable process within the company and to make entrepreneurship a legitimate part of our company's structures and processes. We need to make sure other people can innovate in the future.

So don't get caught up by a preliminary success and forget there is still work to do. It's time to leverage the positive buzz around your early wins to build a repeatable process inside your company.

Chapter 6

REPEATABLE PROCESS

Nine ways to create space for innovation

There is one mistake I would like to stop you from making straight away. Most intrapreneurs I work with are just waiting for the moment when they can negotiate for a physical space of their own – away from the mother ship. I have observed that some intrapreneurs spend an inordinate amount of time negotiating with leadership for such a physical space (i.e. an accelerator or innovation lab). When they get it, they work hard to make the space a great place to work: bean bags, whiteboards, table football, sticky notes and stand-up desks.

Now that you have some credibility within the company, you may be thinking this is your moment to do the same. But if you do this, you will be reverting to innovation theatre. Being given a physical space for innovation does not mean that you have been given space to innovate within the company. Don't waste the goodwill you have earned from an early win by fighting for a physical space for your team. You will need to fight just as hard for nine other spaces for innovation:

1. *Space in strategy:* This involves working with leadership to make innovation an explicit part of corporate strategy. We should work with our leaders to help them think about the future and how the

company is going to use innovation to respond. Leaders can then make clear decisions about what the company will (and will not) focus on with regards to innovation. Such a clear innovation strategy is great because it makes it easy for intrapreneurs to choose to work on projects that they know matter to the company. Strategic alignment also creates an explicit commitment from leaders that if we find a great new business model, they will invest in taking it to scale.

2. *Space in budget:* Leaders need to protect their investments in innovation from budget cuts. If funding can be cut at any time, innovation projects are less likely to have sustained success. Teams will be constantly fighting for their existence. Beyond financial investments, innovation also needs people and their time. It is impossible to sustain innovation if we do it in small bits of time in between our day jobs. So we need to create a space for innovation whenever leaders are allocating budgets, people and time.

3. *Space in portfolio:* We need to create space for new innovations within our company's portfolio of products and services. It is relatively easy for leaders to invest in incremental improvements

REPEATABLE PROCESS

to current products. Growth innovation, where companies make new products for new markets or develop new business models, is much more difficult to accomplish. As such, we need to help leaders decide on the portfolio balance that we want to achieve as a company (i.e. explore vs. exploit). In this process, we have a way to create portfolio space for new value propositions and business models.

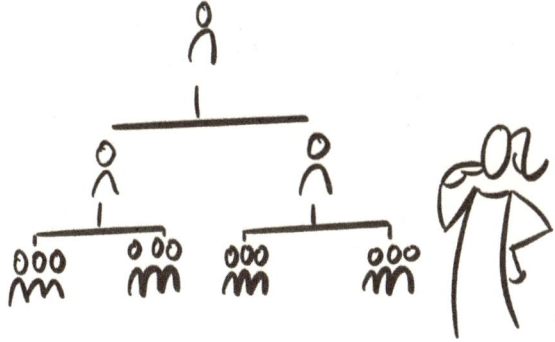

4. *Space on the organisational chart:* Contemporary innovation teams use lean startup methods that involve experimentation and iterative product development. This new way of working cannot be managed using the same leadership styles, processes and tools we use for managing our core products. This is why innovation needs its own space within the organisational

structure. Our role as pirates in the navy is to create a legitimate space for innovation on the company's organisational chart.

5. *Space to collaborate:* There should be a bridge for collaboration between innovation teams and the core business. As pirates in the navy, we have the advantage that we can use the company's market presence, customer base and brand to drive our innovation projects. If the company won't let us do this, there is little advantage to our intrapreneurship efforts. If we are not collaborating with the core business, we are effectively a startup in chains.[21] We have to create the space to collaborate with the core business.

---

21   An argument that my colleague Alex Osterwalder often makes.

REPEATABLE PROCESS

6. *Space for incentives:* Human resources matter when it comes to innovation. We have already discussed the importance of people and their time. Innovation teams also need to have the right incentives in place. Within our HR management systems, there are rules on how bonuses and incentives are calculated. We need to create a space for innovation among those rules.

7. *Space for tools:* Over the last few years, innovators have developed some wonderful tools for innovation. Design thinking, agile, lean startup and business model design tools are now widely available. The acceptance of these tools within our organisations is something we have to achieve. We need to create a space for innovation tools within our company, so they can have equal status to the tools used to run the core business.

8. *Space to fail:* We cannot use rigid business planning for innovation. About 80 per cent of new product ideas will fail. But the more things we try, the more likely we are to find something that works. This means that intrapreneurs need a space to fail and learn. We need a flexible innovation process that allows for experimentation and testing. We must create a space and management process that embraces and celebrates failure and learning.

9. *Space to learn:* Innovation requires people to learn new skills. There is no point getting resources and time if we are not going to use them well. Most people in established companies are used to working in traditional ways. As such, we need to create spaces for learning. As innovators, we need to train our colleagues across different departments on the new ways of working (e.g. lean startup and design thinking). This will be useful later when we need their support for our growing number of projects.

As you have probably gleaned, the above nine spaces are exactly aligned with the innovation readiness model I presented earlier in Chapter 4.

In my opinion, these are more important than a physical space. They are fundamental to our effort to create a sustainable innovation

REPEATABLE PROCESS

process. If we end up with a physical space, it should only act as an expression of these nine spaces. In fact, if you can have these nine spaces within your company, you may not even need to set up a separate physical space. You will have succeeded in creating an authentic space to innovate.

But getting the spaces for innovation is a difficult task because it involves difficult leadership decisions. This further highlights why the early win is just an initial step. You will now need to leverage your new-found street cred to create a lasting innovation process and engage in stakeholder management.

Why every company needs a repeatable innovation process

In every large organisation I work with, at some point we get into a contentious conversation. I keep saying they need to be more innovative. The more I say this, the more executives in the room get annoyed. After some back and forth, one executive inevitably says something like: 'We don't have a problem with innovation. Remember last year we launched that digital platform or application thing? That was a great success, right?'

Of course they are right. There are very few companies on the planet that are totally devoid of innovation. The question is not whether they can innovate every now and again, but whether they can go beyond the one-off projects and include innovation as a sustainable and repeatable process.

What is different across companies is the number of hoops that employees have to jump through to get innovation done. As you may have learned on your way to getting that early win, intrapreneurs have to be long-suffering and patient diplomats to get any new products developed or launched. It often takes a combination of tenacity, brute force and political skills that most people just don't have.

The real question that underlies my conversations with leaders concerns what happens when low-ranking employees have great new product ideas that could result in revenue growth for the company. Is there a clear and repeatable process that employees can follow to explore their ideas, test key assumptions and take successful products to market? Or is innovation success more of a hit-and-miss?

Most companies are not innovation ready. So most employees

with good ideas have no clear place to start. And in the process of figuring out what to do, there is a risk that in every conversation with leaders and managers the idea will be killed. Since you now have the credibility to do it, it is your job to build a repeatable process for innovation within your company. This is what innovation engine building is all about. I bet you wish you had taken the blue pill now.

In order to build a great innovation process, you will need to develop a clear understanding of what it takes to move from idea to profitable business model. Your experience with early adopters should also inform your understanding of how such a process would work inside your organisation. The innovation framework you are about to develop is now your product. You have to make sure that it resonates and makes sense inside your organisation. In order to be effective, the repeatable process you design should accomplish the following:

- *Remove obstacles:* By doing discovery work and starting small, you will have developed an understanding of what is getting in the way of innovation inside your company. The process you design should, at a minimum, remove obstacles such as lack of leadership support, long business cases, ROI expectations and minimise the impact of annual budget cycles.

- *Incremental resources:* As already noted, teams need protected funding for innovation. You need to design a process that describes how this funding will be released to innovation teams incrementally. Small amounts of money can be released for intrapreneurs to test their ideas through experiments with customers. These funds can be released without the need for long business cases. If intrapreneurs show progress towards a profitable business model from their experiments, then more funding can be released to them.

- *Provide guidance:* The process you design also needs to provide clear guidance on how to get the funding for innovation. What types of ideas is the company looking to invest in? What amounts of budget and resources are available? How are intrapreneurs expected to use those resources? What are the expectations for running experiments? What are the success criteria for receiving the next incremental batch of funding?

- *Right expectations:* Innovation is often stifled by leaders who ask the wrong questions at the wrong time. The innovation process you design should guide leaders on how to set the right expectations. For each stage of the innovation process, leaders should be asking the right questions. For example, during the early stages of the project, leaders should not be asking about future revenues. Rather, they should be asking about risky assumptions and what the teams are doing to test these.

Our goal is to move beyond innovation as a one-off process where companies create only one or two new products every three years. We are going to create a repeatable process for turning creative new ideas into profitable businesses. Your challenge now is to identify and remove all the unnecessary hoops that employees in your company are having to jump through to innovate. You now need to view your work much more seriously than you may have done before. You are in the process of creating the missing function inside your company.

The missing function

When we started doing this work, our goal was to make innovation a legitimate part of the organisation. Our dream was to have innovation appear as a legitimate part of the company's organisational structure. We know that our company needs to create a number of innovation teams to test and develop new business ideas. The challenge we are tackling is that these teams need distinct management structures and processes to support them. But whose job is it to develop and manage these innovation structures and processes?

In the majority of companies, there is no function that is responsible for entrepreneurship. Therefore, developing entrepreneurship as a management function is our aspiration. This is not as lofty as it sounds. In *The Startup Way*, Eric Ries observes that it wasn't that long ago when marketing, HR and finance were not official functions within large companies. The management challenges of the twentieth century drove the creation of these functions inside businesses. It is clear to me that the most important management challenge of the twenty-first century is sustaining entrepreneurship within large, established companies. So we need to build up this missing function.

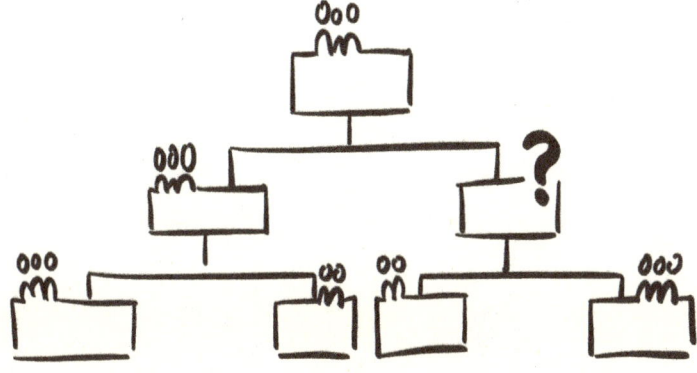

The Entrepreneurship Function

At its core, the entrepreneurship function is responsible for ensuring that the company innovates on a continuous basis. More specifically it is responsible for helping the company develop its strategic guidance, management systems and toolbox for innovation.

A company's culture is determined by what it celebrates, rewards and/or punishes. Creating an innovation culture that recognises failure as the key to learning is the job of the entrepreneurship function. The entrepreneurship function also needs to create tools that help leaders make decisions about what to do with successful startups or startup teams. Do we scale them internally? Do we create new divisions? Do we spin them out? Do we sell them or shut them down? Do we build, buy or partner?

Once these management systems are in place, the entrepreneurship function is then responsible for maintaining and continuously improving the process and tools. Ultimately, when leaders and teams ask us the following questions, as outlined by Eric Ries,[22] we should be able to answer convincingly:

- How do we create the space for experiments with appropriate constraints?
- How do we fund projects without knowing the return on investment in advance?
- How do we create appropriate milestones for innovation teams that are working autonomously?
- How do we provide professional development and coaching to help people get better at entrepreneurship?

---

22 Ries, E. (2017). The Startup Way. New York: Penguin.

- How do we create cross-functional teams with the right people in them?
- How do we create the right incentives and advancement systems?
- How do we manage and transition successful startup teams?

I am confident that there will be more questions to answer, but our task is clear. We are now working on creating the missing function. As we move beyond early adopters, into the early majority and the rest of the company, we will need to become a more buttoned-up operation, carefully organised and operated. We need to provide our teams and leaders with good tools and processes that support innovation. It's an exciting mission and I hope you will enjoy being a part of it.

Embedding the right practice

Before we develop any innovation management process, we need to have a clear understanding of what the goal of the process is. If we are unclear about this, we are likely to design a process that is not fit for purpose. For example, I have worked with innovation teams that have designed a process that is optimised for generating a lot of creative ideas, but is not optimised for testing those ideas to find the right value proposition and business model.

I have previously defined innovation as the combination of creative ideas and sustainably profitable business models. This means that, beyond generating a lot of ideas, innovation teams should spend time searching for the right value propositions and business models. But what exactly are they searching for? To make it more concrete, it is helpful to think of 'searching' as a process for answering four key business model questions.

Desirability – Should This Be Done?

While generating breakthrough ideas is a good start, the question still remains whether there is anybody in the real world who cares about the product or service we are thinking of creating. What problems are we solving and for which customer segment? Is there a real customer need out there? How do we reach these customers? It is often hard for innovators to accept that customers don't really care how clever they are. Customers care about their own problems and aspirations. As such, the best way to create value propositions that resonate is to develop a deep understanding of those problems and aspirations.

Feasibility – Can This Be Done?

This question speaks to the technical risks in any innovation project. Will we be able to create whatever breakthrough technologies we are imagining? The seriousness of the risk depends on the nature and complexity of the product or service. A number of software products (e.g. apps) do not present that much technical risk. However, for other, more ambitious projects, such as driverless cars, electric cars, healthcare or pharmaceutical products, technical risk is a genuine concern. In other words, in some innovation projects we will still have a lot of work to do to figure out whether the product can be developed at all.

Viability – Can This Be Done Profitably?

In addition to figuring out how to make a great solution for our customers and delivering it to them, we should also spend time figuring out the rest of our business model. Where will we create and deliver value? How will we reach customers to tell them about our product and/or deliver it to them? How much will it cost us to create and deliver value? How much will customers pay? How will we break even or get to profitability? The answers to these questions are key to the survival of our product in the market. Creative breakthroughs can change the world, but this is much harder when you don't have any real traction in the market.

Adaptability – When Should This Be Done?
In *The Wide Lens*, Ron Adner describes a critical blind spot that most companies have when they are working on innovation projects. This blind spot relates to timing. There are often things that have to happen within a company's business environment before a breakthrough product can be launched. To what extent does your product depend on the successful commercialisation of other companies' innovations? Innovators who have ignored these questions have failed by being 'too early'. While you may get accolades as a great inventor, this is no comfort when fast followers come behind you and take over the market. So timing is important. Make sure the external ecosystem is aligned and ready before you go to market.

Understanding the external environment also helps with scaling. Finding a real customer need is not the same thing as finding a market, because it is important to ensure that the customer needs we have identified represent a large enough market for us to make profits. However, finding a great market does not automatically mean we will succeed at scale. It is important for us to figure out our growth engines – the methods by which we grow our customer base – and ensure that as we grow we are maintaining product quality and excellence.

For example, making ice cream in a small kitchen is different from mass manufacturing. It is also possible that the costs of scaling can render our business model unprofitable and unsustainable. All these issues have to be actively identified and resolved if our breakthrough innovations are to reach their full potential.

Doing the Right Thing at the Right Time
In order for an innovation to succeed, the team needs to successfully answer all the questions outlined above. They have to do this by doing the right thing at the right time. The best process to follow is for the team to:

1. Design their business model using their imaginations and the best information they have to hand.

2. Identify the key assumptions that they are making within their business model that are yet to be proven with evidence.

3. Classify these assumptions in terms of the question category they belong to (i.e. desirability, feasibility, viability and adaptability).

4. Prioritise these assumptions in terms of their importance to the success of the business model.

5. Run experiments to test each assumption, use lessons learned to iterate on business models until they find something that works.

This is the best practice that all good innovation teams follow. They don't skip steps because each step matters for success. Doing the right things at the right time means we ensure that our ideas become sustainably profitable business models over time. As such, the process we develop for our company should support these best practices. It should guide teams through the searching process and also allow leaders to track team progress while making good investment decisions.

The innovation process

Understanding the key questions that innovation teams have to answer provides us with a structure through which we can develop our innovation process. The moment that innovators hear the word process, they often start rolling their eyes. Process, as a management concept, has a bad reputation. Rigid processes have been accused of stifling innovation, and in my experience this is true. Corporations tend to stifle creativity when they manage innovation using the same processes they use to manage their core products.

But this is not the fault of process as a management concept. It is important for us to distinguish between good and bad processes. There is, after all, a difference between the baby and the bathwater. An innovation process is only as good as the assumptions about innovation that informed its design, and how well those assumptions map to reality.

Traditional management processes are based on often faulty assumptions about the stability of the world. This is why most management processes are generally unresponsive to change (e.g. annual budgeting). Often these assumptions are implicitly held within the company, which makes it hard to improve the process if it becomes problematic. In most of these situations, process can become a bottleneck that leads to unproductive decision-making.

When it comes to managing innovation, these traditional assumptions have to be challenged. The goal is not to get rid of process altogether, but to design better and more responsive processes. I still believe that innovation is management. It is not merely creativity – but a systematic process for finding business models that work. This is not to say that, if we design a good innovation process, it has to be blindly followed. A good innovation process should be different from other processes, and designed to evolve based on the learnings we've made.

There are several innovation processes that have been designed and published. Examples include Steve Blank's Customer Development[23] and Ash Maurya's Running Lean.[24] These are all great processes for managing innovation. However, I recommend that companies create bespoke processes that are appropriate to their context. Having discovered a lot more about your organisation as part of your innovation journey, tailoring the process should be relatively easy for you to do.

A good innovation process should help innovation teams navigate uncertainty. More importantly, it should help teams to do the right thing at the right time. For example, before creating a solution it is important to first understand our customers' needs. Before spending money on a huge marketing campaign, it is sensible to ensure that we have found the right channels. Before scaling, it is important to make sure that we have a profitable business model. Doing the

---

23 Blank, S., & Dorf, B. (2012). *The startup owner's manual: The step-by-step guide for building a great company*. *California: KS Ranch.*
24 Maurya, A. (2012). *Running lean: Iterate from plan A to a plan that works. California: O'Reilly Media.*

right things at the right time is key for successful innovation and our innovation process should support that.

The Lean Product Lifecycle

From 2014 to 2019, I was part of a team at Pearson that designed an award-winning innovation framework – the Lean Product Lifecycle (i.e. Lean PLC).[25] Our framework had six stages. The first three stages were focused on searching for a profitable business model: *idea, explore, validate*. The last three stages were focused on executing a known business model: *grow, sustain, retire*. The Lean PLC was based on the principle that no product or service should be taken to scale until we have found a profitable business model. First, we search – then, we execute. Each stage in the Lean PLC is described below:

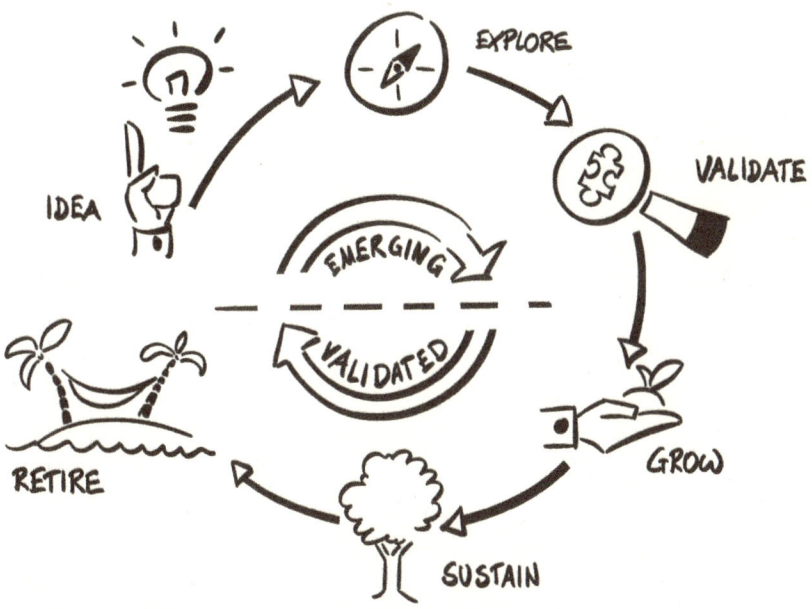

---

[25] Viki, T., Strong, C., & Kresojevic, S. (2018). *The Lean Product Lifecycle: How to Make Products People Want*. London, Pearson.

- *Idea:* Teams generate ideas or explore new technologies. However, the critical part of this stage is when the team designs their business model, reviews it for risky assumptions and brainstorms, ways to test these assumptions.

- *Explore:* Teams get out of the building and test their assumptions about customer needs, problems and jobs-to-be-done. The critical question here is desirability. Do we have real customers, with problems we can solve, who are looking for and willing to pay for a solution?

- *Validate:* Teams develop a solution for customers, starting with a minimum viable product. The point is to test whether we can create a solution that delivers value to customers (i.e. feasibility). The solution development process is also used to test other parts of our business model, such as how much it might cost to create and deliver the solution, whether we need any key partners, the right channels to reach and acquire customers and how much customers might be willing to pay (i.e. viability).

If a team successfully makes it to this point, they have found a profitable business model. Only then are they ready to scale and move to the other side of the Lean PLC.

- *Grow:* The main focus during the grow phase is to test the adaptability of our business model. The key question here is whether we can grow customer numbers, revenues and profits.

- *Sustain:* As our product or service matures in the market, it reaches this stage of the Lean PLC. The goal here is to sustain current revenues and profits, while optimising operations and reducing costs.

- *Retire:* When the product is in decline, it should be retired from the portfolio. The main thing to keep in mind here is that we don't want to inconvenience customers as we retire our products – so retirement should be managed well.

The Lean PLC was implemented within Pearson as the product development process for innovation and managing core products. I present it here as an example of a process you could develop for your organisation. You can also take elements from this process and redesign it for your own company context. I have done this myself several times for many companies.

The most important thing to remember is that you must design the process so that innovation teams can generate ideas, identify assumptions and test those assumptions using the right tools. The process should also be designed so that teams can make decisions based on evidence. There is no point in testing our assumptions if we then fail to use our learnings to make informed decisions. A good process should allow teams to change direction based on what they have learned, and stop the project if they need to, without negative consequences for them. If this is not possible, then our process is simply innovation theatre.

Investment decision-making

As noted earlier, one of the biggest myths around innovation is that good returns require companies to make large investments. The problem with making such big bets is that leaders then need to make sure bets. This is where the long business cases come from. Leaders feel they need as much information as possible on day one before they can make decisions.

The problem with huge bets is that once a team gets their million-dollar investment from the board, they are not necessarily going to be disciplined enough to do the right things at the right time. Instead, they are going to take the money and execute their plan. I have met a lot of innovation teams who have blown through their budgets, launched a flawed product and are now struggling in the market. This is why the innovation process we design has to be linked to how we make investment decisions.

> *No innovation team gets a large budget to build and launch at scale before they have tested and validated their business model.*

In order to encourage the right behaviours, we have to use incremental investing or metered funding. We begin by making small bets that then increase over time to those teams that are showing progress towards a profitable business model. At Pearson, the Lean PLC was driven by an investment framework that invested no money for the Idea stage, less than £50,000 during Explore and less than £250,000 during Validate. Only in the Grow stage did teams get a large investment based on their validated business model's P&L spreadsheet.

At each stage, incremental funding should be connected to an expectation that innovation teams will provide evidence of progress. These requirements can be based on the four key factors of desirability, feasibility, viability and adaptability. For example, within the Lean PLC, the £50,000 investment for the Explore stage was connected to an expectation that the team would find evidence of a real customer need facing a large enough market (i.e. desirability). If they failed to provide this evidence, they would not get follow-on funding to enter the Validate stage.

This approach uses investments as the carrot to drive the right behaviour from both leaders and innovation teams. Leaders can stop asking for long business plans. There is no need for it because now they are making small bets. In turn, innovation teams earn more investment by showing evidence of progress. As you design your process, you are going to have to make decisions about the number of stages in the process, what teams are expected to do and how much investment funding they will get at each stage.

Connected to this are the templates that the teams will use to make investment requests. Instead of using the traditional business case, we can create our templates based on the innovation process we have designed. This means that there isn't one generic template that applies to each innovation stage. Rather, the templates should ask the relevant questions for each stage. These questions should represent the criteria to be satisfied in order to move a product from one stage to another. For example, who are the customers and what are their needs? This in turn tells the product teams what they should be doing during any particular stage – which is the ultimate goal of our innovation process.

The innovation process is your product

As the team that is driving transformation, the innovation process you have just designed is your own. Everything you do from now on will be organised around this process. This is the main product you will be selling to the rest of the organisation. Just as finance has processes around how to manage budgets, pay expense claims and report on ROI, you have been designing a process for how to take innovations from idea to profitable business.

The way you design your innovation process will impact a lot of the choices you will make going forward:

- The tools you will choose and recommend for each innovation stage.
- The skills training that you will provide throughout your company.
- The innovation playbook and guidance you will create for innovation teams.
- The templates you will create for the team to provide updates and make investment requests.

- The types of investment boards you will set up, their charters, guidelines and ways of working.
- What you will ask for in terms of budget from the company.
- The financial process you will set up for incremental investing.
- The communications between the innovation teams, leaders and the executive board.
- The adoption roadmap for the company and how various business divisions will implement the process.

This is why we have to take great care in designing our innovation process. Just as with any product, we should not design our innovation process within a vacuum. We have to test the process with leaders, product teams and other key stakeholders inside the company. As we apply the process, we should iterate based on feedback until we find something that works.

Everything we do from now on hinges on having a conceptually sound and robust innovation process. So we have to get it right. We have to build our process iteratively in collaboration with colleagues in the business. I am sure you can now see why having good relationships with key stakeholders really matters. You cannot do this on your own. You will need help from some catalysts.

Chapter 7
THE CATALYSTS

You can't do this on your own

When I outlined the importance of doing discovery work within your company in Chapter 4, one of the things I emphasised was the need to speak to key stakeholders. Now that you are designing and trying to implement an innovation process, stakeholder relationships become even more important. I have worked with innovation teams that felt they could bully their way through the organisation because they had support from the CEO. This is a grave mistake to make.

You cannot take an aggressive approach to driving transformation – especially if the goal is to drive innovation. In this work, our goal is to change mindsets. It is a play for people's hearts and minds. As much as she may have power and influence inside the company, the CEO's mandate does not carry the same force as a supreme court ruling.

I once witnessed an interesting exchange between a CEO and an innovation team at a Strategyzer event. The team were pitching to the CEO an idea for an accelerator program to incubate startups within a company. During the pitch, the team said that they would provide updates to the CEO once every quarter. Surprised by this, the CEO advised the team that if they waited to see him once every three months, several managers would already have come to see him repeatedly over that period to complain about the accelerator program.

Beyond this difficulty of dealing with stakeholders who don't support our work, we also need to get active help from those stakeholders who do support our work. It is no good to have them cheering us on from the sidelines. The innovation process we have designed cannot be implemented effectively without their active involvement.

For starters, we cannot implement an innovation process in a business division that is unwilling to adopt it. So we would need to work closely with the leadership inside those departments. We will also need support from other stakeholders such as:

- *Human resources:* for the creation and incentivisation of innovation teams.
- *Technology:* for the creation of a sandbox for teams to experiment safely with applications.
- *Finance:* for access to investments, budgets and resources.
- *Legal and compliance:* for guidance on how to innovate within the rules.

These are just a few examples of the stakeholders we will need to work with. We cannot do this alone, and we will need to work collaboratively with others. These people are our catalysts. If we work with them well, they will increase the pace with which our company adopts the innovation process we have designed.

The early majority

When we began our transformation program we worked with early adopters. These are the leaders who understand that the world is changing and are acutely aware that their company needs to innovate. They have been actively looking for solutions, have sponsored some internal innovation activities, have the resources and budget to invest, and they are prepared to make a time commitment towards innovation.

But we cannot scale our process using just early adopters. Sure, the early win was nice, and it feels good to hang out with people that agree with us. However, we were working with early adopters as a bridge to the main business. We now need to move to the early majority. These people are not pioneers. They will not try things that they have not seen others do successfully. They need to know that things work before they adopt them.

They will often lack two or more of the characteristics that define early adopters. Most early majority leaders understand that the world is changing all the time and that their company needs to innovate to stay successful, but they may have strong doubts about whether innovation can be done at all within their organisation. As such, they may not be looking for solutions or have any resources set aside to invest in innovation. Some leaders may have resources that they are willing to invest in innovation but are unsure how to make investment decisions or manage the innovation process.

The early majority are different to early adopters. These leaders will not tolerate our mistakes or allow us to use their divisions to 'learn'. They are looking for things that work. This means that we now have to be more organised in how we work with their divisions. We now need to think of ourselves as a proper entrepreneurship function that delivers value to the company. We need to have our tools, methods and processes ready to go.

This is why we need to work with organisational catalysts. When we show the early majority that our process has support from leadership, finance, legal and HR, we will easily get their buy-in. They won't feel they are going against the grain in the company. So who are these catalysts and how do we work with them?

The leadership

Leaders are perhaps the main catalyst for any corporate innovation process. While having executive-level support will not solve all our problems, not having executive-level support means that our innovation process is dead on arrival. Remember what we are trying to do here: we are trying to change the company so that innovation becomes a legitimate part of our company's structures and processes. We have absolutely no chance of transforming the company if we fail to secure some level of leadership support for our work.

THE CATALYSTS

Leadership support is so fundamental to innovation, I am surprised how many innovators try to ignore it. Just imagine trying to be a pirate in the navy without having to work with the admirals. Sure, you can try to run an underground innovation movement inside your company. But this is not very different to what was happening before. Furthermore, underground movements have a high mortality rate. Eventually, you will have to come up for air and resources, and it is then that the leadership in your company will notice you. Your survival rate then depends on how those leaders respond to your work.

This is also the reason why lean startup training is not enough. We can train people all we want. However, the reason they can't use that training inside our company organisation is that their managers will often not allow them. Just giving people innovation skills is of no value if those skills are not going to be used. I was once caught up in a dispute between an intrapreneur and their manager. The intrapreneur was insisting on testing the product with customers but the manager wanted it launched as soon as possible. This conflict got so personal that the intrapreneur eventually quit the company and joined a startup.

This just shows that, without leadership air cover, you can only go so far. So now is the moment to take your time to meet with key leaders in your company to ensure that you have their full support. The political campaign can begin in earnest. Get your beautiful PowerPoint presentation ready. You have your early win. Now it's time to tell your story to executives and get their support.

You will need to share with leaders a general roadmap for implementing your innovation process. Use this roadmap to be honest with your leaders about the long-term nature of the project. Furthermore, be explicit about the type of support you will need. Make sure you get clear commitments from leaders, preferably in writing. Do not settle for a fudge or ambiguous commitments. For example, don't accept it as success when leaders say: 'Just get started and we will give you more support after we see how it goes.'

Ask them why they can't give you that support now. What you are looking for is active support, something that is visible within the organisation. In one company I worked with, we managed to convince the Chief Financial Officer to write a blog post to the whole company endorsing our new innovation process. Not only did the CFO do this, he also insisted that no innovation projects would get funding or budget without following our innovation process. This was a highly valuable feather in our cap. It helped to unlock a lot of difficult conversations with middle managers.

The ultimate proof of leadership support is when things get difficult. In the example above, we experienced challenges from managers trying to circumvent the innovation process, who would go directly to the CFO and plead for funding for their projects. We initially lost these battles, but over time more and more leaders began to push teams through our innovation process.

Ultimately, you will not get support from every senior executive in your company. It is enough to get support from two or three leaders who will commit to giving you the protection you need. Of all the senior executives inside your company, you need to make sure you get support from the CEO and/or CFO. If neither of those two will make this commitment, then you may have real problems.

I still need to repeat here that getting top-level support does not give you licence to go for a big bang. You still need the discipline to make sure that you are starting small and doing the right thing at the right time. Do not use a CEO/CFO endorsement to ride roughshod over people and push through your agenda. Instead, seek to create more goodwill for your innovation process across the company by working with other stakeholders and catalysts.

The investment board

With leadership support, you can start to think a bit more about investment decision-making. If you recall, our innovation process requires that we make incremental bets using metered funding. To

ensure that innovation teams do the right things at the right time, we invest a little and then increase investment in those teams that are showing success in finding a business model that works.

A key question we have to answer concerns who is responsible for making these incremental investments in innovation projects. While it is possible for individual leaders or managers with the budget responsibility to make such decisions, this is not what you want. You want to make incremental investment decision-making in innovation an institutionalised practice within your company. You don't want it happening in small pockets of the organisation.

When we implemented the Lean Product Lifecycle at Pearson, we pioneered the concept of product councils. These were investment boards comprised of leaders and managers who used metered funding to make incremental investments in products and services. The product council included staff from:

- Finance
- Legal and Compliance
- Sales and Marketing
- Technology
- Operations
- Design
- Branding
- Heads of divisions

For investment boards to be effective, they need to balance two things. They need to have a senior enough membership that is allowed to make meaningful budget decisions within the company's schedule of authority. At the same time, they need to be close enough to the innovation teams in order to make quick and informed decisions. If the members of the board are too senior, they will not know enough about the innovation projects to do this. They will also be too busy to meet often. This will create a bottleneck for teams that need quick decisions.

One assumption we can't make at the beginning is that senior leaders already know how to ask the right questions and make the right decisions around innovation. Left to their own devices, leaders tend to fall back on traditional criteria such as return on investment (ROI). As such, when we set up our investment boards, we will need to train them to make decisions using our criteria.

The enablers

Successful innovation results from the combination of great ideas with profitable business models. No innovation team can bring a new product or service to the market on their own. The complexity of innovation requires collaboration among all the key functions within an organisation. When Apple was launching the iPod and

iTunes, this required coordination with manufacturing for creating the product, marketing for selling, technology for writing software, legal for contracting with record labels and many other divisions. This is why we have to work with the so-called enabling functions. We have to get alignment with the key functions at our company, if we are ever going to be able to scale our innovation process within the organisation.

Let's think about the journey of a product or service from idea to scale. Let's see who might get involved in the process and how:

- *Executive leadership:* for defining strategy and deciding that this idea is something the company should focus on.
- *Finance:* for budgets and other key resources.
- *R&D and technology:* for breakthrough ideas and technical support.
- *Manufacturing and operations:* for producing the product and ensuring delivery to customers.
- *Human resources:* for recruiting new team members and deciding on the right incentives.
- *Marketing and sales:* for selling the product through various channels and managing customer relationships.

There are several other key functions that I have left out of this, including branding, legal and compliance. But I hope that you get the point I am trying to make. You need to work with all these key functions for success. This is why it is important that they are all aligned around the same innovation framework.

When we were working at Pearson, one of the first teams we tried to align with was finance. We viewed this as a key driver in the Lean Product Lifecycle process. As such, we spent a few months working with finance to create an incremental investment framework they were comfortable with. Ultimately, we succeeded in agreeing a ceiling spend for each product lifecycle stage. They also agreed to create for us a new financial template for when teams were ready to take their ideas to scale.

In another scenario, I was working with a company in the financial sector. In this industry, compliance with regulations is really important and we spent time working to align with legal and compliance. Over a series of workshops, we developed an understanding of the requirements that they needed before a product was taken to scale. We then worked through how those requirements could be adjusted based on the innovation stage of a product. The goal was to achieve a legal and compliance process where the requirements were lighter for early stage products but then got heavier as the teams made progress towards full-scale launch.

The work to align with enablers is perhaps the most important in terms of catalysing innovation projects. I have seen good innovation projects stalled because of a legal or procurement issue. However, if there is alignment between divisions within an innovation process, there is minimal friction for innovation. Then projects can more easily flow through the necessary steps.

The coaches

Part of building innovation practice inside a company is building up the skills of employees. I have worked with companies where teams have the opportunity to work on innovation projects but they lack the right skills to do so. They don't know how to design a

business model, identify assumptions or run the right experiments to test their ideas.

The other challenge that most employees face is time. Most people working in large companies do not have enough hours in their working week to build up the right skills for innovation. So when they start working on a project, they are unsure what to do. This is where coaching can really help. When employees have limited time, surrounding them with the good innovation coaches can help move projects forward.

One option for companies is to use external consultants as coaches. This is good practice and can help to build up credibility. However, this option is expensive and often fails to help companies develop their own internal innovation skills. This is why, ideally, every company needs its own group of internal coaches.

At Intuit they train internal coaches through a program called Catalyst. They recruit internal coaches and train them on their Design for Delight innovation process (D4D). As Kaaren Hanson, the former VP of Design Innovation, noted in a *Harvard Business Review* article: 'We not only needed people who were design thinkers – we also needed people with passion to give D4D away and help others to do great work.'[26]

Remember I said earlier that your innovation process is now your product. This is similar to the D4D process in Intuit, where they train people to coach the D4D process. At Pearson, our Train the Coach program trained people to coach the Lean Product Lifecycle. The process involved:

1. *An introduction webinar:* Where we covered lean innovation principles, the six stages of the Lean PLC and expectations around the program.

2. *A two-day workshop:* Where we dived deep into the Lean PLC and how to coach innovation teams.

3. *Coaching practice:* The coaches were then required to coach a few teams on business model design, experiment design and Lean PLC decision-making.

4. *Six webinars:* These webinars provided a check-in where the coaches could get support while they were working with their teams.

After completing this process, the coaches became Certified Lean PLC coaches. We recruited coaches from all over the business, who were then deployed to help teams there. This allowed the process

---

26   Martin, R.L. (2011). 'The Innovation catalysts', Harvard Business Review: https://hbr.org/2011/06/the-innovation-catalysts

we had developed to not only belong to us, but to have passionate advocates spreading the word and helping teams to succeed.

The community

It is important that we don't just work with each group of catalysts in isolation. What we are trying to do is create a movement. So we need to turn our catalysts into a community of innovation practitioners. We need to create a range of possibilities for them to interact with and learn from each other. Creating a community gets rid of isolation and provides a great subjective norm for innovators (i.e. I am not alone in this company – there are others like me).

As such, we should start building a community by organising regular meetups where people can share best practice. These meetups can also feature external speakers and a weekly coffee or

lunch. People can turn up, select topics and discuss their challenges and successes.

Beyond actually meeting, we can also use digital tools to create a community. For example, we could host weekly or monthly webinars where we discuss various innovation topics. We can also create a digital platform with blogs, videos and an interactive page.

Our goal is to have a dynamic community that works together to create a buzz within the company. This is why we might want to open some of our events and platforms to people who are interested in innovation but are not coaches or catalysts. We may now even consider hosting company-wide events such as hackathons and idea competitions. As long as these are all linked to scaling our innovation process, we will be building support and momentum.

Chapter 8

SCALE THE MOVEMENT

The late majority

Depending on the size of our company, it may take over a year before we complete our work with the early majority. How quickly our innovation process is adopted by the company depends on two main factors. First, how professional are we as an entrepreneurship function? Do we have all our tools and methods ready? Do we work collaboratively with other key functions in the business? Second, what is the cultural appetite for innovation within the company? I have worked with organisations where adoption was slow and methodical. I have also worked in companies where adoption was quick and enthusiastic.

Whatever the case may be, at some point we will begin working with the late majority and perhaps even the laggards inside the company. These people come to the party quite late. They tend to be conservative and sceptical and will only join our movement if they have no choice. So while our work with early adopters was to gain the credibility to attract the early majority, our work with the early majority is to build an irresistible momentum for our movement that makes the adoption of our tools by the late majority and laggards a fait accompli.

If we find ourselves still publicly justifying our existence when we begin engaging with the late majority, then we have not succeeded as a movement. We may need to rethink our strategy. Having a repeatable process that is supported by a strong network of catalysts should create the momentum that drives adoption among the late majority and laggards. Of course, having momentum does not mean that we should force the late majority and laggards to adopt our process. We are still going to have to work collaboratively with them and win their hearts by showing them how our innovation process helps them succeed.

Flexible roadmap

In Chapter 5, I recommended resisting the allure of long-term planning. I argued that during the early stages of transformation, we should not be making detailed plans and roadmaps for our project. Our focus should be on learning and responding to our company's needs. However, we are now at a different stage in the process. We have succeeded long enough to be working with the late majority.

At this point, we should have discovered quite a lot about how our company operates. We should also have learned what works with regards to business divisions adopting our innovation process. It is time to codify those learnings and create a roadmap or milestone tracker.

As we design this roadmap, we should always remember that companies are organic living things that will respond to our

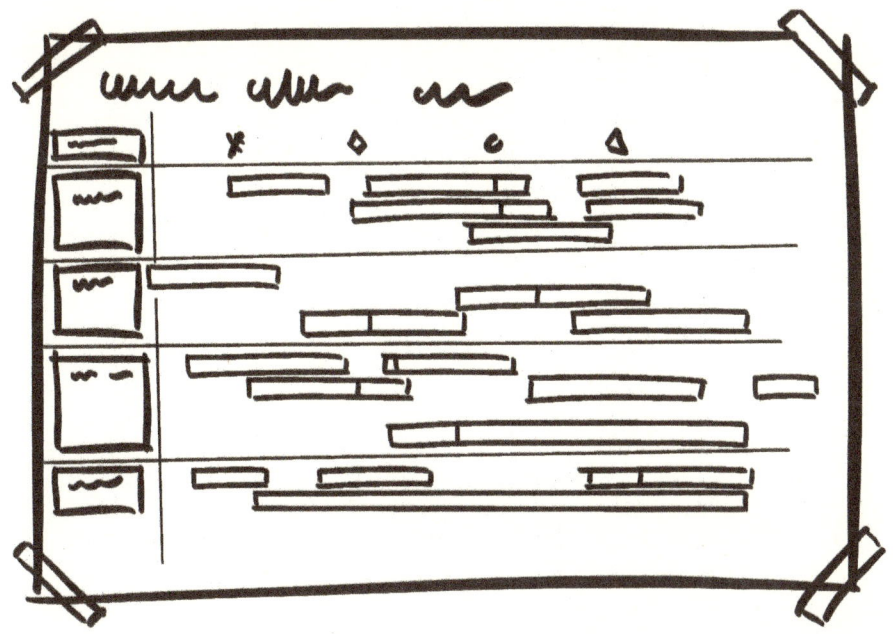

interventions in unexpected ways. Regardless of our experience, the best transformation plans will generally not survive their first contact with the organisation. We will need to work in a way that allows us the flexibility to respond to the unexpected. The best way to do this is to:

1. Start by defining the end goal for each engagement we will be having with business divisions in the company. What does success look like? For example, if we are trying to create an innovation board within the organisation, success may be defined as persuading the board to meet to make investment decisions, using the right innovation tools, at least once every month. We can set similar goals for working with innovation teams, coaches, catalysts and leaders.

2. After defining the end goals, we can then identify the key milestones that will need to be achieved in order to reach that

ultimate goal. For our innovation board example, a key milestone may be that the CEO has to identify and confirm the chair of this board and also appoint the key members. Another milestone may be the training of this board to use the right tools to make decisions, with the ultimate milestone being that the board has its first meeting. Again we can set similar milestones for our work with innovation teams, coaches, catalysts and leaders.

3. We then need to create a dashboard to track these milestones. This is not a Gantt chart with dates and a roadmap. Rather, this tracks how much progress we are making towards the goal. In my experience, it is hard to predict exactly what will happen when a business adopts our innovation process. This is because, while we are working on the nuts and bolts of the adoption, we are also working on the human side by trying to get buy-in from the people we are working with. It is the human side of transformation that is messy and hard to roadmap. As such, we should create our dashboard as more of a milestone tracker that tells us what we have accomplished so far, and what still remains to be done.

As we develop our roadmap, it is important that we don't confuse implementation with adoption.[27] Several companies that implement enterprise software are then surprised to find out that most of their employees are not really using it. The difference between implementation and adoption is around people's relationships with the tools. To the extent that people don't see value in our tools,

---

27 Dickie, J. (2009). 'Don't confuse implementation with adoption', Destination CRM: https://www.destinationcrm.com/Articles/ReadArticle.aspx?ArticleID=53684

we can implement them all we want, but they will not necessarily adopt them.

So what we are looking for, as we roll out our innovation process, is evidence of adoption. We are looking to see whether the company is changing at a cultural level. The best evidence of this is the behaviours people consistently display. So as we set our goals and milestones, we should focus far less on our own activities as a team, and focus more on the behaviours we are hoping to see within the business. This way our dashboard becomes an adoption tracker rather than a roadmap.

Create a playbook

An important part of scaling our innovation process is to create a playbook that leaders and teams can use to drive their innovation projects. The truth about working inside large organisations is that we cannot possibly train everybody. But even if we did accomplish such a feat, attending workshops does not mean that people are ready to drive innovation within their company. They will need coaching and reminding about the things they learned in the workshops.

This is when the playbook becomes handy. It is a way to bring our innovation process to life and make it practical for teams. The best playbooks are visual and provide clear guidelines on how to practise innovation. At Pearson, we created a playbook that eventually became a book entitled *The Lean Product Lifecycle*. We used our innovation process as the framework to guide how the playbook was organised.

For each stage of the Lean Product Lifecycle, we described the relevant tools and how they can be used by teams to achieve success. For example, at the beginning of the playbook, we guided teams on how to design their business models and extract key hypotheses. During the Explore stage, the playbook provided clear guidelines on how to talk to customers and gain meaningful insights.

The goal of the playbook is to help teams do the right things at the right time. Therefore, it is also important to show within the playbook how the outputs of each innovation stage are connected to the investment decisions that leaders will make. It is also key to show teams how their progress towards success will be evaluated and measured. Ultimately, the goal is to help teams find value propositions that resonate with customers and business models that generate profits.

Align innovation with business strategy

Another important part of making sure we are able to scale our innovation process is to align it with business strategy. This alignment matters a great deal. One of the innovation myths I identified in

Chapter 1 is this idea that innovation is partly about making a thousand flowers bloom. While it might be true that we want to make a lot of small bets before we find something that works, we also want to make sure that we are making these bets in a strategic way.

In an innovation benchmark report published in 2017 by PricewaterhouseCoopers, they found that 54 per cent of the leaders they surveyed struggled to bridge the gap between innovation strategy and business strategy.[28] They also found that 65 per cent of companies that invest over 15 per cent of their revenue in innovation indicated that aligning business strategy with innovation was their top management challenge. Fifteen per cent of revenue. That is a lot of money being invested in innovation projects that are, in essence, flying blind.

I strongly believe that such seemingly random acts of innovation do not always result in great returns. Companies should not be investing in an arbitrary collection of unrelated innovation projects.

---

28 PricewaterhouseCoopers (2017). PwC's Innovation benchmark report. https://www.pwc.com/us/en/services/consulting/innovation-benchmark-findings.html

There has to be some connection between our innovation strategy and the company's overall business strategy. This is particularly important if we ever want our new ideas to get investment to scale in the market.

I was once in the United States working with an innovation team at one of the large financial institutions in the Midwest. They had invited me to help them craft their strategic guidance for choosing innovation projects to pursue. During our meeting, one member of the team explained to me why they had decided to do more work to clarify their innovation strategy. When they first started working on innovation, they used to call themselves the home for homeless ideas. They viewed themselves as the place where people with ideas that the main business did not want to work on would come for support. They would nurse these 'unwanted' ideas and give them resources. Sounds like a great role for an innovation team, right?

Well, the intrapreneur I was speaking to made one statement that speaks to the fallacy of the separate and independent innovation lab. He said:

After a while, we realised that if an idea is homeless when it gets here, it will be homeless when it leaves.

This is why it is important that intrapreneurs align with their leadership in terms of the strategic goals for innovation. We need to make sure that we are working on ideas that have a good chance of being taken to scale by our company. We don't want our innovation process to ever be the home for homeless ideas. To define our strategic guidance for innovation, we have to engage with leaders to:

1. *Assess where we are as a company:* What products and services do we currently have in our portfolio? What capabilities do we have as an organisation? Which of our business models are under threat of disruption from startups and competitors? Which innovation projects are we currently running and how much progress are they making?

2. *Assess our business environment:* What is going on in the world around us? What key trends should we be paying attention to? Are there emerging technologies we should be concerned about? Are there fledgling startups or competitors that could disrupt our business?

3. *Identify key gaps:* Is our current portfolio of products, services and capabilities adaptive to its business environment? Where are the gaps in our portfolio?

4. *Define strategic guidance:* How are we going to use innovation to respond? Which key trends should we be exploring? Which moves are we going to make in order to improve our portfolio of products, services and capabilities? Which new business models and value propositions are we going to invest in?

Working with leaders to define this strategic guidance is important. But even more important is making sure that our innovation process is aligned to this strategy. The more we are seen by our leadership as a vehicle to help the company fight disruption, the more likely we are to sustain the momentum we have created.

Aligning incentives

The final piece in scaling is working closely with the human resource department to align on incentives. One of the myths around innovation is that creative people do not care about being rewarded for their work. That all you need to do is give them a space to work and they will be happy. While it is true that innovators are often driven by some great cause, this does not mean that they don't care about reaping the rewards for their work.

If innovators repeatedly create million-dollar products and services for their company, eventually they will become tired of winning the annual innovation award (a gift card). It is important that we work with HR to recognise the contributions of innovators to the company. One thing we could set up is a process through which innovators get a percentage of the revenue they create via bonuses. Another option is to spin out startups as separate companies in which the intrapreneurs are shareholders. Depending on the complexity of our situation, we can choose the right model to use.

Another key conversation to have is to create innovation as a career path within the company. Most companies don't have innovation as part of their organisational chart. To make it easy for people inside the company to choose to innovate, it has to be clear what the career path is. This path must begin at the lowest levels inside the company, move through middle management and all the way to the C-suite. If there is no leadership presence for innovation at the top level, then it will be hard to sustain it long term within the company.

Finally, we need to work with HR to create incentives for leaders to allow their teams to innovate. This goes beyond the incentives for the teams themselves and the career path inside the company. At this level, we are trying to remove the barriers that middle management often create for their teams. If these managers are only rewarded for managing the core business, then they will constantly get in the way of their teams and drive them towards working on the core products and services.

One option that you could use is to adopt the 3M company's approach to setting stretch goals[29] – which are challenging and ambitious. For example, you could set up a process through which leaders receive their bonuses if 20 per cent of their revenues come from new products launched within the last four years. This will communicate the importance of innovation to leaders, and align their incentives to those of the innovation teams.

To the Future…

And beyond! The goal is to embed innovation as part of the company. We do not want to undertake one-off innovation projects and

---

[29] William E. Coyne (2001). 'How 3M innovates for long-term growth,' Research-Technology Management, 44:2, 21-24, DOI: 10.1080/08956308.2001.11671415

constantly have to protect our ideas from leaders. In other words, we want the navy to embrace piracy as a way of doing business. But if that happens, are we really still pirates? This is an interesting question that I will discuss in the concluding chapter.

Conclusion
NOT ALL PIRATES ARE THE SAME

This book has explored how innovators can become pirates in the navy. From the beginning, my goal has been to destroy the notion that innovators should view the company they work for in an antagonistic way. Instead, what we want to do is make innovation a core part of how our company does business. This led me to the conclusion that although this book may be about pirates, not all pirates are the same.[30]

Terms like pirate, privateer and buccaneer are often used interchangeably. While all three words describe pirates, they do not mean the same thing. The difference between pirates and privateers is most important for this book.[31] A pirate is a person who commits theft at sea. This involves attacking ships, often without discrimination. In other words, a pirate is essentially a criminal.

In contrast, a privateer was a pirate who had been granted a licence by a government to attack and steal from ships belonging

---

30 This idea was hatched over dinner with Shachaf Snir – a leading Isreali innovator and thinker.
31 In case you are interested, a buccaneer is a French term from the seventeenth and early eighteenth century that was used to describe pirates or privateers operating in the Caribbean.

to an enemy government.[32] This licence, also known as the 'Letter of Marque', meant that when the privateer returned with the proceeds of their adventures, these would be shared between the government, the ship owners and the privateer. In other words, a privateer had backing from their government to do the work.

Their status rose higher when privateers secured commissions to become explorers. Privateers like Sir Francis Drake and Sir Thomas Cavendish would get commissions from their governments to explore foreign territories and claim some of them for their home countries. This meant that when they returned with their findings, there was interest from their governments to further invest in the enterprise.

---

32 Whitenton, B. (2012). 'The difference between pirates, privateers and buccaneers Pt 1', The Mariners' Museum and Park: https://www.marinersmuseum.org/blog/2012/09/the-difference-between-pirates-privateers-and-buccaneers-pt-1/

NOT ALL PIRATES ARE THE SAME

This is where the difference lies for pirates in the navy. If you are just a pirate, then the leaders inside your company do not really care about what you are working on. If your idea is discovered, it will be made to walk the plank. But if you are a privateer or an explorer, the leaders in your company have vested interest in your success. This is because they have essentially commissioned the work you are doing. As such, the innovation projects you work on are much more likely to get the support they need to succeed.

How to get the commission to be a privateer or explorer is what this book is about. This is not easy work. There can be a lot of political inertia inside established companies, particularly large ones, and any efforts at transformation may trigger resistance. But if we succeed in getting our commission, we will have made innovation a legitimate part of our company. This is the transformation we are working towards. We want to work in a company that is good at both managing its core business and exploring new opportunities.

Epilogue
AN UNDERGROUND MOVEMENT

What I have been describing in this book is a process for how intrapreneurs can move from the peripheral edges of their company, to become a legitimate part of how the company does business. It is a process for how to move from being a pirate who works on stuff that nobody else in the company cares about, to being an explorer who creates new products and services that are aligned to the company's innovation strategy.

But this is not an easy task. It is perhaps one of the more difficult things to attempt inside an established company. After doing some discovery work, you may actually learn that it is going to be extremely difficult to transform your organisation. The leadership

may be too entrenched in their old ways of working. I am often asked by intrapreneurs about what they can do if they fail to find any early adopters among their company's leadership. My advice is always the same. Quit!

However, if you insist on staying in the company then I will offer you different advice. Run and hide! It is now time to start an underground movement. If you want to innovate in a hostile environment, you will need to use guerilla tactics to protect and nurse your ideas until they are strong enough to come out into the open. Below is a brief survival guide, adapted from Tristan Kromer,[33] that you and your team can use to navigate the treacherous territory of corporate politics:

1. *Lower cost of innovation:* Whatever you do, do not spend a lot of money or resources on testing your ideas. In an underground movement, the cost of testing ideas should be negligible. You need to master lean startup tools and use them effectively. You also need to move quickly. The longer you take to test, the more chances there are for leaders to discover your ideas and kill them. The goal here is to gather enough evidence as quickly as possible about their viability so that when we are found out, we can make a compelling case to be allowed to continue.

2. *Stay away from the company brand:* I once worked with a team that made the mistake of sending out an email brochure to customers to test whether their value proposition resonated. In the email, they provided their details for anyone who was

---

[33] Kromer, T. (2014). 'Lean Startup + Enterprise = Lean Enterprise': https://grasshopperherder.com/lean-enterprise-innovation-ecosystems/

interested in the offering to contact them. They thought that this move would contain the blast radius of the experiment as customers would only get in touch with them if there was some interest. But this is not what happened.

What they forgot to consider was that a lot of these customers already had good relationships with the sales team inside the company. So after receiving the email, instead of calling the team using the details provided, the customers called their sales representatives. As you can expect, the sales team were totally unaware of this 'new product' being tested. After the Head of Sales heard about this experiment, the team was in a lot of trouble. Their idea was almost killed and they were lucky to keep their jobs.

The key lesson from this story is that you should stay away from the company brand, and, more importantly, from their current customers. By opting to run an underground movement, you have effectively forfeited your access to the company brand. So use a white label or a fake brand name to test your value propositions and take your ideas to new customers rather than the company's current ones. Only later, when you have more evidence of traction, can you hope to get permission to use the brand.

3. *Get a separate space:* As you may have gathered already, I am not a fan of the innovation lab that is physically apart from the company. However, this might be an option for a team that is working within a hostile environment. So if you can swing it, get yourself a separate space. Preferably as far away from the mother ship as possible. If you can get located in a different city, even

better. If it was up to me, I would choose a cool city like my native Harare, or Cape Town, San Francisco, Amsterdam, London, Berlin, Shanghai, New York.

4. *Get a separate budget:* In addition to getting your own space, you need to get a separate budget. It is difficult to run an underground movement if you have to depend on a middle manager for budget approvals every quarter. In my experience, the best budget option is to be part of an R&D team. It is often the case that R&D investments are amortisable. It is easier to run an underground movement if you show up as an amortisable expense rather than an operational cost. Again, the goal here is to find ways to go unnoticed within the company. We only want to be noticed when some of our ideas have undeniable traction.

5. *Find a diplomat:* Finally, you will need to find a diplomat. You need to have a key ally among the leadership team to provide you with some air cover. This diplomat has to be both well connected and well respected inside the company. Their role is to support your work, get you budgets and resources, buy you time for experimentation and protect you from the bureaucracy of the mother ship. Their role as a bridge to the company becomes even more important if any one of your ideas succeeds. When it's time to ask for resources to scale your ideas, there is nothing more valuable than having a well-respected leader in your corner.

Just one last piece of advice. When you are running an underground movement, remember to keep it quiet. Once you talk about it, it's no longer an underground movement. If you want to be famous or

AN UNDERGROUND MOVEMENT

popular within your company, you've chosen the wrong movement. You have to be extremely patient and care about the success of your ideas more than anything else. If you make too much noise with your ideas by demanding resources and attention too early, your movement is more likely to fail. Good luck to you – I wish you the very best. But I sure don't envy you.

Index

accounting rate of return (ARR), 33
Adner, Ron, 123
Airbnb, 41
Amazon, 98
Apple, 62, 145
architectural innovation, 42–3
assumptions prioritisation map, 96

behavioural change, 102–3
Blank, Steve, 1, 22, 33, 88, 126
brainstorming, 9
branding, 4, 18, 38, 81, 85, 144, 146, 172–3
bridge to the core, 72
business model canvas, 95–6
business model lifecycles, 41–2
business models, profitable, 9, 16, 18, 23–4, 33, 44, 48, 63, 117–18, 121–8, 130, 145
    key questions, 122–3

career paths, 164–5
Catalyst program, 148
Cavendish, Sir Thomas, 168
challenger banks, 47
Christensen, Clayton, 35, 45, 60
Clark, Kim, 42
coaches, 147–50
cynicism, 53

decision-making, 34–5, 37–8, 46
Design for Delight (D4D) process, 148–9
detractors, 89–90
diplomats, 174
disincentives, 36–40, 58–61
doubt, 53
Drake, Sir Francis, 168

early adopters, 75, 82, 88, 90–6, 98–101, 104, 117, 121, 155, 172
    compared with early majority, 139–40
early majority, 139–40, 155
early wins, 97–105
enablers, 145–7
entrepreneurship function, 120–1
executing vs. searching, 22–3, 33

failure, 35, 39–40, 114
finance, 4, 73, 81, 85, 119, 132, 138, 140, 144, 146–7

Financial Times, 42
Forbes magazine, 54
Ford, Henry, 82

Gantt charts, 87, 158
growth vs. transformation, 48–50

hackathons, 92
Hanson, Kaaren, 148
Henderson, Rebecca, 42
human resources (HR), 4, 73, 81, 85, 113, 119, 140, 164–5
humility, need for, 57–8, 64

idea competitions, 9, 92
incentives, 72, 164–5
incremental investment (metered funding), 62–3, 143
inertia, 52
innovation accounting, 33–4, 46, 97
innovation activity map, 77–8
innovation awards, 164
innovation boards, 157–8
innovation community, 150–1
innovation engine building, 48, 50, 77, 117
innovation fatigue, 21–2
innovation labs, 12–21, 29–30, 90, 109
    and PR, 19–20
innovation mapping, 76–9
innovation myths, 7–10, 160–1, 164
innovation orphans, 64–6
innovation paradoxes, 2–3, 32–6
innovation practice, 72–3, 94
innovation process management, 73, 125–33
innovation silos, 14, 64–5
innovation strategy design, 94–7
innovation theatre, 10–12, 76
innovation tools, 73, 94–7, 113
internal resistance, 29–30
Intuit, 148
investment decision-making, 46, 94, 130–2, 143–5

Jacoby, Ryan, 49
Jobs, Steve, 1, 17, 58, 62

Kodak, 41, 43
Kromer, Tristan, 172

laggards, 155–6
late majority, 155–6
leadership, 70–1, 140–3, 145
leadership deficits, 36, 64, 171–2
Lean Product Lifecycle (Lean PLC), 127–31, 144, 146–7, 149, 160
lean startup, 7, 15, 17, 19–20, 29, 44–6, 59, 73, 82, 91, 111, 113, 172
    training, 44–5, 141
learning from experience, 74–6
legal and compliance, 4, 81, 85, 138, 140, 144, 146–7
Letters of Marque, 168
long-term planning, 87–8, 156
loss aversion, 89

management
  innovation process management, 73, 125–33
    management structures, 119–21
    management tools, 46–7
    managing innovation, 31–2, 58–61
    portfolio management, 47, 71, 94, 110–11
Maurya, Ash, 126
Merkazy, Ran, 99
metered funding (incremental investment), 62–3, 143
middle managers, 58–61, 79–82
Musk, Elon, 57–8, 61, 74

net present value (NPV), 33
Newman, Daniel, 54
Nintendo Wii, 9
Nokia, 41

organisational structures, changing, 42–4

patience (and impatience), 35–6, 69
PayPal, 9
Pearson, 127, 129–30, 144, 146, 149, 160
perceived norms, 102–3
'permafrost', 59–60
personal digital assistants (PDAs), 9
pirates (the term), 167–9
playbooks, 159–60
portfolio management, 47, 71, 94, 110–11
PowerPoint, 98, 142
PricewaterhouseCoopers, 161
privateers, 167–9
process alignment, 65–6

repeatability, 116–18
return on investment (ROI), 33, 145
Ries, Eric, 119
roadmaps, 156–9

Samsung, 99
Silicon Valley, 17
skills development, 73
software development, 38–9
space, 109–15, 173–4
SpaceX, 58
stakeholders, 30–1, 75, 79–82, 98, 115, 133, 137–8, 143
startup accelerators, 12–13, 19–21, 109, 138
    see also innovation labs
startup founders, former, 81
stock markets, 89
storytelling, 103–4
strategic goals, 7, 13–17, 30–1, 37, 59–60, 157–63
Strategyzer events, 137
Strategyzer tools, 95–7
stretch goals, 165
survival guide, 172–4

test and learning cards, 96–7
3M company, 165
Train the Coach program, 149
transformation, barriers to, 51–4
transformation planning, 85–8
transformation vs. growth, 48–50

Undercover Economist, 42

value proposition canvas, 95
venture capital, 8

Xerox, 41, 43

Unbound is the world's first crowdfunding publisher, established in 2011.

We believe that wonderful things can happen when you clear a path for people who share a passion. That's why we've built a platform that brings together readers and authors to crowdfund books they believe in – and give fresh ideas that don't fit the traditional mould the chance they deserve.

This book is in your hands because readers made it possible. Everyone who pledged their support is listed below. Join them by visiting unbound.com and supporting a book today.

David Alick
Mirko Bahrenberg
Greg Bernarda
Jonathan Bertfield
Robyn Bolton
Jonathan Bradshaw
Reggie Britt
Paul Brown
Roberto Chaverri
Jeff Chen
Andrea Cocchi
Damien Evrard
Andreas Frei
Nicholas Hartley
Louise Heywood
Phil Hornby
Yanitsa Ilieva
Bill James
Stefan Jungmayr

Dan Kieran
Steffen Knodt
Tanja Kufner
Cyril Lamblard
Rachel Lawlan
Matthias Leistikow
Maurice McGinley
John Mitchinson
MT
Thor Olsen
Eduardo Pinilla
Justin Pollard
Mary-Kate Portley
Daniel Ross
Christoph Sander
Daniel Santa Cruz Prego de Oliver
Chad Schaefer
Heino Schaght
Justin Souter

Kai Springwald
Bart Suichies
Thinkers50
Nicolai Nehammer Thorsell
David Trayford

Kumaran Veluppillai
Vincent Vierhout
Ute Wellenberg
Matt Wood